Introduction

This book contains absolutely nothing of any value and none of the advice therein should be taken seriously.

Editor-in-chief, Academic Advisor and Chief Administrator: Sir Ramick Hobbs M.D., Ph.D., D.Sc., M.A.

WHY IS PUBIC HAIR CURLY?

Vernon
Coleman

BLUE
BOOKS

Small Print

Parts of this book previously appeared under the title *The Complete Guide to Life* and the authorship of Edward Vernon. The book has been issued in this new form in order to confuse librarians and bibliographers.

First published in 1995 by Blue Books, PO Box 30, Barnstaple, Devon, EX32 9YU, England
Reprinted in 1996

ISBN   1 899726 03 9

A catalogue record for this book is available from the British Library

Printed and bound in the UK by J W Arrowsmith Ltd, Bristol

Warning

The percentage of humour in this book is not enough to satisfy the normal daily requirements of a deranged adult according to figures laid down by the World Health Authority in 1981 and revised by Lynton & Lynmouth Lacrosse & Hurling Supporters Club Social Committee in 1987.

Note

This book contains the following ingredients:

History: 0.1%
Rumour: 17%
Irony: 24%
Heavy sarcasm: 2%
Ethnic humour: 12.5%
Crude sexual innuendo: 65%
Sociology: 0.04%
Prejudice: 14.8%
Error: 99.99%
Political satire: 1.05%
Plain fact: 0.0%
Fancy fact: 87.6%
Nuclear physics: 0.3%
Vitamin E: 33.8%
Saturated fats: 0.5%
Exaggeration: 12.6%
Wishful thinking: 2%
Folklore: 9%
Myth: 4%
Dirty bits: 69%

If the total does not add up to 100% this is probably due to the author's inability to operate a calculator properly.

Additional warnings to the humour-impaired

- DO NOT TAKE ANY NOTICE OF ANYTHING IN THIS BOOK
- DO NOT FOLLOW ANY ADVICE IN THIS BOOK
- IGNORE ALL INSTRUCTIONS IN THIS BOOK
- PUT THIS BOOK DOWN AND READ SOMETHING ELSE

Curriculum

ACADEMIC MODULE ONE

Tellurian Structure and Somatology

A basic introduction to fundamental biology

Know your own body

Basic anatomy and physiology

HOW DO WRINKLES DEVELOP?

Human bodies consist of hard bits (called bones) and soft bits (not called bones). There are also runny bits such as blood, cerebrospinal fluid, lymph and catarrh. Some bones are long. Others are much shorter. Some are very odd shapes indeed and defy description. The soft bits come in all sorts of shapes and sizes. All this stuff is kept in one place by an envelope made of skin. Because of a basic design fault the envelopes are always too big for the contents. Wrinkles develop when the skin envelope isn't filled properly. If you have wrinkles then you need to eat more food and get fatter. Once you've got enough fat inside your skin envelope, your wrinkles will disappear.

WHY IS PUBIC HAIR CURLY?

Back in the days when elastic was still uninvented and when zips and buttons were almost unobtainable, primitive people used to have quite a job keeping their loin cloths in place. Lots of people got embarrassed if their loin cloths fell off when they ran about. Because of this, pubic hair evolved to become curly and so possess a Velcro-like quality.

WHAT DOES BLOOD DO?

Blood's most marvellous quality is its unique capacity to expand on contact with the air. If you make holes in your skin blood will get out and you'll be able to see this action at work. A teaspoonful of blood will expand so much that it will completely stain a tie, a shirt, a pair of trousers, a jacket, an overcoat, a hat, a carpet, six paper tissues, a linen tablecloth, an oil painting, a lawn mower, a blanket, a dress, a pair of socks, a car rug, a finger stall, a clock and an acre of grassland. A tablespoon of blood can make even more of a mess.

WHY ARE MEN MADE IN A DIFFERENT WAY FROM WOMEN?

Women were designed to make beds, wash clothes, cook dinners, bake cakes, scrub floors, keep the garden and the kitchen tidy, iron shirts, fetch the children from school, write thank-you letters, buy Christmas decorations, look after drunks at parties, drive cars for inebriated husbands, look sexy, fill stockings, warm slippers, light cigars and pipes, polish golf clubs, steam hats back into shape, put hems on curtains, feed cats, do all the shopping and decorate houses.

Men, on the other hand, were designed to sit around and watch television, drink alcohol, play darts, snooker, football, golf and dominoes, smoke pipes and cigars, drive cars too fast, whistle at women, earn money, buy presents, shout at referees, eat cholesterol and vomit on the stairs.

You don't have to be an anatomist to realise that these two sets of activities require different types of body.

WHY DO WOMEN HAVE BREASTS?

Female breasts were designed to make calendars more interesting. Without breasts no one would look at calendars and people wouldn't know when to go on holiday.

WHAT'S IN A BODY?

The average male human body contains:

Seven gallons of rainwater
A pinch of zinc
One puppy dog's tail
Quite a lot of brain
½ oz snails
1½ lb of cholesterol
1 oz of iron filings
2 oz slugs
A little bit of malted barley

The average female human body contains:

Five gallons of rose water
A good handful of sugar
4½ oz of titanium
1 oz of molybdenum
3½ oz of assorted spices
1 small glass of green chartreuse
2 oz peach skin
A little bit of fat
Quite a lot of Vitamin E

ARE YOU MR AVERAGE?

Studies undertaken by the Joint Working Party (Anthropology) of the World Health Authority have enabled scientists in Geneva to ascertain the physical characteristics of the average or 'mean' man. These figures were obtained after the Joint Working Party had measured 22,943 males between the ages of 18 and 65.

Distance between two nipples: 25.4 cm

Distance from right nipple to upper edge of right knee cap (standing): 65.2 cm

Distance from right nipple to upper edge of right knee cap (sitting): 46.4 cm

Distance from left nipple to upper edge of left knee cap (standing): 63.9 cm

Distance from left nipple to upper edge of left knee cap (sitting): 44.8 cm

Area of head hair: 0.73 sq meters

Average length of each head hair: 6.93 cm.

Hair colour: dark blond

Eye colour: sort of greyish, greenish blue

Length of penis (limp): 14 cm

Circumference of penis (limp): 7.6 cm

Number of testicles: 1.996

Length of penis (firm): 28.9 cm

Circumference of penis (firm): 15.3 cm

Length of nose: 2.4 ins

Angle of nose: 47 degrees

Distinguishing marks: small mole on left buttock and teeth marks on right shoulder.

Circumference of head (measured at eyebrow level): 58.7 cm

Length of index finger on right hand: 9.633 cm

Likelihood of length of index finger of right hand being exactly one third of length of firm penis: 89%

Number of hairs on chest (must be above umbilicus and between nipples): 7

Length of hair on chin after 7 days of uninterrupted growth: 0.48 cm

Distance between ears (measured in a straight line): 20.2 cm

Width of mouth (maximum) 4.9 cm

Are you Mrs Average?

Similar studies undertaken by the Chief Medical Officer of the Joint Working Party (Anthropology) of the World Health

Authority have provided similar statistics concerning the physical characteristics of the average or 'mean' woman. These figures were obtained after the Chief Medical Officer had personally measured 23,697 women between 19 and 22.

Distance between two nipples (lying): 44.5 cm
Distance between two nipples (standing): 22.6 cm
Distance between two nipples (sitting): 22.7 cm
Number of hairs round left nipple: 3
Number of hairs round right nipple: 4
Circumference of left breast (maximum point): 30.5 cm
Circumference of right breast (maximum point): 28.6 cm
Weight of left breast (measured by water displacement): 238 grammes
Weight of right breast (measured by water displacement): 227 grammes
Distance from clitoris to left nipple (standing): 45.2 cm
Distance from clitoris to left nipple (sitting): 29.5 cm
Distance from clitoris to right nipple (standing): 46.3 cm
Distance from clitoris to right nipple (sitting): 28.4 cm
Height of clitoris (min): 0.3 cm
Height of clitoris (max): 2.7 cm
Depth of vagina: 0.87 index fingers
Distance between eyebrows: 2.3 cm
Area covered with pubic hair: 26.4 sq cm
Distinguishing marks: small brown freckle on left lower outer quadrant of left breast
Hair colour: light black
Eye colour: a sort of blueish, greenish grey
Width of mouth (maximum): 11.5 cm
Distance between ears (measured in a straight line): 20.1 cm
Angle of nose: 55 degrees
Length of nose: 2.1 ins
Volume of left breast: 1.3 standard handfuls★
Volume of right breast: 1.14 standard handfuls★

★According to regulation 467CD/25j the Chief Medical Officer's hands are of standard size.

HOW TALL SHOULD YOU BE? (MEN)

If you weigh	Your height should be:
126 pounds	5 feet 10 inches
133 pounds	5 feet 11 inches
140 pounds	6 feet 0 inches
147 pounds	6 feet 2 inches
154 pounds	6 feet 4 inches
161 pounds	6 feet 8 inches
168 pounds	6 feet 10 inches
175 pounds	7 feet 0 inches
182 pounds	7 feet 2 inches
189 pounds	7 feet 4 inches
196 pounds	7 feet 8 inches
203 pounds	8 feet 0 inches
210 pounds	8 feet 6 inches
217 pounds	8 feet 9 inches
224 pounds	9 feet 1 inch

HOW TALL SHOULD YOU BE? (WOMEN)

If you weigh	Your height should be:
112 pounds	5 feet 4 inches
119 pounds	5 feet 6 inches
126 pounds	5 feet 8 inches
133 pounds	5 feet 9 inches
140 pounds	5 feet 11 inches
147 pounds	5 feet 12 inches
154 pounds	5 feet 14 inches
161 pounds	5 feet 17 inches
168 pounds	5 feet 23 inches
175 pounds	5 feet 28 inches
182 pounds	5 feet 33 inches
189 pounds	5 feet 38 inches
196 pounds	5 feet 43 inches
203 pounds	5 feet 54 inches

What you can do if your height/weight ratio is wrong

1   Walk around on tip toe, or put things in your shoes.

2   Try stretching exercises. Have all your kitchen shelves moved up until they are almost out of reach. Put your TV set on a special shelf ten feet above the ground. Have your car seat moved back so that you can hardly reach the wheel. Marry someone taller.

3   Buy very tight clothes. Wear two girdles. Your body will be compressed, but since Einstein's law of close relativity operates here your body will remain constant. With a narrower girth you will inevitably get taller.

4   Lie about either your height or your weight.

Physiological Status Enhancement

An introductory course in health maintenance

Basic preventive medicine

There was a time when disease was more or less confined to the Far East and parts of Northern England. With the advent of modern methods of travel, illnesses have spread alarmingly. It is now possible for almost anyone to contract diseases, despite the quarantine laws that apply to foreign nationals.

We print here a list of essential do's and don'ts designed to help you avoid contamination.

1 Never eat raw foods.
2 Don't mix with strangers.
3 Always wear gloves when dealing with mail, reading newspapers, books or magazines. Always wear spectacles when reading tabloid newspapers.
4 Don't take stimulating drinks (such as alcohol, tea, coffee, cola, cocoa, drinking chocolate, milk shakes etc.).
5 Don't eat foodstuffs that have been cooked.
6 Wash your whole body in antiseptic at least 4 times a day.
7 Make sure that your nurses wash the enema syringe in disinfectant before use.
8 Only make love to sterilised partners.

Diet and the Gee Plan

Alphonse Gee of the Dietetics Department at the Nice Polytechnic has published a series of paper which have shown conclusively that, eventually, we all look like the food we eat. To help his clients mould their bodies according to their desires, Dr Gee has produced a special eating plan.

If you want your body to develop more curves you should eat plenty of:
>oranges
>apples
>bread rolls
>grapefruit
>melons

If you want to flatten your stomach you should eat plenty of:
>pancakes
>omelettes
>plaice
>sliced bread

If you want to become stronger you should eat plenty of:
>raw meat (yuk)
>mussels
>stilton cheese
>curry

If you are male and you want to improve your sex life you should eat plenty of:
>big sausages (vegetarian only)
>bananas
>carrots
>rhubarb
>cucumber

If you are female and you want to improve your sex life you should eat plenty of:
>figs
>oysters
>stuffing

Breast examination

IMPORTANT NOTE: This examination is designed to help relax the examiner. It is of no value whatsoever to the owner of the breasts.

1   The breasts to be examined must be naked. (Otherwise there is a risk that you might mistake a buckle or strap for a lump.) It is best to remove all clothes down as far as the waist. When this has been done the breasts can be examined visually. They should be viewed from several angles.

2   With the supporting chest wall in the vertical plane, cup the left breast in your right hand. Now carefully assess the weight of the breast. Move your hand up and down slowly as you would if the breast were a melon and you were a potential customer. Do this for three minutes.

3   Use your left hand to assess the right breast. Do this for three minutes.

4   Now return your attention to the left breast. Gently stroke the nipple with the thumb of your right hand. The nipple should respond to this procedure by increasing in size, thus facilitating examination.

5   Use your left thumb to stimulate the right nipple.

6   Cup the right breast again with your left hand. Assess for another two minutes.

7   Cup the left breast once more with your right hand. Assess for an additional two minutes.

8   Trace a circle around the right nipple with the forefinger of your left hand. Do this at several levels as though you were drawing contours around the breast. You should be able to manage eight or nine contour lines on an average sized breast.

9   Repeat this exercise on the left breast.

10 Cup the right breast again with your left hand.

11 Cup the left breast again with your right hand.

12 Use your left thumb to stimulate the right nipple.

13 Use your right thumb to stimulate the left nipple.

14 Trace contours on the right breast.

15 Trace contours on the left breast.

16 Now repeat procedures 1 – 15 with the owner of the breasts in a reclining position.

17 Now repeat the whole breast examination procedure with the owner of the breasts in a kneeling position where the torso is horizontal and supported by the owner's outstretched arms.

18 The breasts should be examined at least once a day in this manner. In the hands of a skilled examiner the whole procedure should take no more than sixty minutes.

Get taller by racking your brains

The height of the human body (or length if the body in question is lying down) is dependent on the distance of the brain from the other bits and pieces. Clearly, therefore, any process or procedure which increases this distance will add to the individual's height (or length).

In the past people have tried to increase their height (or length) by physical methods such as muscle stretching, bone transplantation, or wearing shoes with lifts. It is now recognised, however, that these primitive techniques are far inferior to more sophisticated cerebral solutions.

Many previously short individuals have now provided solid evidence that it is perfectly possible to increase one's height with a deliberate 'racking of the brains'. The technique involved is fairly simple and consists of a short series of quantified isonumismatic movements. Here they are:

1 Begin by trying to visualise the blood vessels connecting the heart, lungs and kidneys to your brain. Visualise the blood corpuscles setting out merrily on their short day-trip.

2   Next try to visualise those blood vessels getting longer and longer. Imagine the corpuscles packing for a long journey and expecting to spend a week or a fortnight away from home.

3   By practising this exercise four times a day for six or nine months you will be able to increase the distance between your brain and the other organs. This is what 'racking the brains' really means.

4   With the blood vessels becoming longer and the major organs further from the brain, the muscles, bones and other paraphernalia will have no alternative but to increase in length as well.

5   The average individual should be able to increase his height or length by some four to six inches in a year.

Sharpen your eyesight

Lots of people who wear spectacles and contact lenses, or who use magnifying glasses in everyday life, could manage perfectly well without them if only they would learn how to sharpen their own eyesight. Artificial aids are usually quite unnecessary after one four-hour session. Here is what you need to do:

1   Remove any spectacles, contact lenses or other aids.

2   Go outside and look into the distance. See as far as you can.

3   Now try and imagine that you can see the people who are standing in the fields, streets and parks which make up your 'distance'.

4   Now pretend that you are standing with those people.

5   Now look into the distance and try to see as far as you can. You're still standing in your original position, but you think you're standing in the spot where you can imagine people standing and so now you're seeing over twice as far as you can really see. And you've only been practising this tech-

nique for a few seconds!

6   Continue with this exercise. Imagine that you are standing in the place where you imagined that you think you can see people standing. Now try and look into the distance.

7   Within twenty minutes you should be able to see right round the world.

8   Within an hour you'll be looking at the back of your head.

Removing excess hair

Excess body hair can be a terrible embarrassment. There's nothing worse than going into the public swimming baths and having people stare at you because you've got hairy legs, hairy armpits or hairy tufts escaping from the lower edges of your bathing costume. Body hair really is quite revolting and it is also very dirty. Lots of strange beasts live in body hair and research has shown that in a square inch of ordinary pubic hair there are probably in excess of twenty eight billion living creatures.

Look in magazines and you'll find that there are lots of companies selling products designed to help you remove excess body hair. You can buy razors, waxes, tweezers and all sorts of weak, chemical defoliants. None of these works well – as a peep in any public swimming pool will quickly show.

The only really effective ways to remove body hair are these:

(a) The powerful chemical XZC-110 was used in the Vietnam War as a defoliant for six years before it was found that none of the Vietnamese who had been sprayed with the chemical ever grew body hair again. You can now buy XZC-110 exclusively from a Peruvian arms dealer whose name I will supply in return for a 500DM note. Simply pour a little on the parts of your body that grow unwanted hair and you'll soon notice the difference.

(b) Ordinary blow lamps are *not* suitable for removing body hair, but the specially produced, nuclear powered JK Major will do the job well and comparatively safely. Under medical supervision aim the lamp directly at the hairs and move it away just as soon as you detect that tell-tale odour of singeing flesh. There will be a small third degree burn where you've used the blow lamp but the risk of hair growing there again is almost negligible. You can only obtain a JK Major by sending a blonde 25 year old woman with a blank cheque to Sir Ramick Hobbs at the address given at the end of this book. Do not use any other kind of blow lamp.

ACADEMIC MODULE THREE

Technical Mothercraft

Motherhood and childbirth: before, during and after

Teaching your unborn child to read

Much advice is given to parents about the birth and postnatal care of children. Little is said of the practical help that can be given before the birth itself. This section begins with one or two useful hints on how to advantage your child in the weeks before its delivery.

The child who is able to read when he comes into the world will have a tremendous advantage. Instead of wasting time with building bricks, rattles and stuffed teddy bears he'll immediately be able to get his gums into the works of literature's giants: Tolstoy, Dickens, Henry James and Mickey Spillane. There is nothing quite so pleasing as seeing your child settle down with a rusk in one hand and a copy of *Time* magazine on the other. Complicated? Not at all. Just follow these simple instructions:

1   You must make sure that your baby is in the head down position. Check with your doctor if you are unsure about this. You should, however, be able to feel your baby's tiny skull resting on your pelvis.

2   Start with a simple, large print alphabet book. However bright he is your child won't be able to cope with Proust

straightaway.

3 Place the book flat on the floor, open at the first page.

4 Stand astride the book (first remove your clothing, of course).

5 Using a pointer, tap the first letter and speak it out loud.

6 Repeat.

7 Proceed through the book to 'Z'.

8 Make this process a daily routine. You won't be able to hear your baby's responses, but with perseverance you'll give birth to a child whose mind has developed along with its body.

Exercising your unborn child

Every mother knows that unborn babies kick and stretch a lot. Few know that those early movements can be controlled to valuable effect. Teach your baby to exercise effectively (instead of with mere random movements) and you'll give him a head start over other infants of a similar age. When he's born he'll have well-developed muscles and impressive coordination.

Start by teaching your foetus the secret of rhythm. Buy a small tape recorder and hold the loudspeaker near to your umbilicus – play music written by such giants of the world of rhythm as Stravinsky. After two or three hours a day for a month or two your foetus should be kicking in time and stretching with the beat. Try Schoenberg for an occasional change.

At this stage you can introduce specific exercises to your unborn child's daily programme. Get a friend to whisper instructions into your umbilicus. Such exhortations as 'one two three, UP two three, IN two three, OUT two three, DOWN two three, UP two three' are eminently suitable. Do remember, however, not to over-tire your foetus. Increase the daily exercise programme gradually.

Who should be at the birth?

Childbirth used to be a very private affair. Selfish young mothers and possessive female relatives would exclude husbands, uncles, friends and genuinely interested passers-by from the more interesting moments. Today, medical opinion suggests that as many people as possible should attend a new baby's arrival into the world.

The grandparents

It is easy for grandparents to feel excluded from the intimacy of childbirth. They, as much as the husbands or boyfriends, have a right to be present in the delivery room.

The bride's former boyfriends

Revolutionary investigations made by Dr Warren Peace of the Institute of Seminal Studies in Leningrad prove that sperm can survive in the vagina for up to ten years. Since this means that fatherhood is difficult to determine with absolute certainty, former boyfriends of the bride obviously have a vested interest in the confinement.

The groom's former girlfriends

Many girls whose former lovers have left them to marry someone else become depressed. Their depression sometimes deepens when they discover that a former lover is about to become a father. The depression might, however, be lifted if they are allowed to see their successors enduring the agonies of parturition.

Interested professionals

In the past only medical students and pupil nurses have been entitled to attend births. It is often the case, however, that people in professional capacities will have to take charge at an unexpectedly premature birth, or officiate when a young mother-to-be has simply delayed getting to hospital. It's essential that such people have as much practical experience as possible. A report by the Dutch All Party Commission on Birth suggested that tram drivers, policemen, traffic wardens, social workers, firemen, milkmen, postmen, grocery van drivers, ambulancemen, bus drivers, taxi drivers, train drivers, coach drivers, bicycle riders, walkers, airline pilots, helicopter pilots, hovercraft pilots, ships' officers and crews, factory workers, office workers, people who work in or pass through public places and people who spend more than 24 hours a year out of their own homes might well benefit by attending a minimum of ten deliveries each.

Neighbours, future babysitters, potential teachers and probation officers

The Swedish socio-psychologist Hans Christian Andersen has shown that if people likely to have close contact with a child as it grows are to enjoy a full and rewarding relationship with it, then they are likely to benefit from being present at the birth. Only then, it seems, will they be able to experience those close emotional ties which are an essential part of what would otherwise be an unrewardingly formal relationship.

NOTE
Since these deliberations show that the average birth needs to be watched by between nine and ten thousand people, the International Birth Observation Society has ruled that home confinements should be made illegal. Hospital delivery rooms are physically inappropriate for the observation of childbirth by so many people, so forward-thinking Governments are busy converting old theatres, bingo halls and churches into delivery observation centres.

Keep a record!

Childbirth is an important social event but one which is often allowed to pass unrecorded. Those important moments can all too easily become a blurred memory. Why not use your video recorder to preserve for eternity the angry screeching and squawking of the midwife, the mother-to-be's laboured breathing punctuated by sobs, cries and screams of pain, the enema and its distasteful consequences, the twang of rubber gloves, the evocative clatter of steel instruments in a steel tray, the harsh glare of fluorescent lighting, the grunts and groans heralding the final stages of labour, the nauseating effect of anaesthetic gases, the dark, ugly bloodstains dampening the green theatre clothes, the clash of forceps blade on unrelenting bone, the agonised yells as tender skin tears and tears again, the muttered oaths half lost in the surgeon's paper mask, the sobs of the new mother mixed with the unhappy whimperings of her infant, and the drama as the surgeon struggles to suture the injured perineum. What memorable images; and so strange that we should forget them so easily.

What to do with the afterbirth

Amazingly, many people throw away the afterbirth or placenta. Even in a world of planned obsolescence this sort of wastefulness is quite reprehensible. Here are three suggestions for ways in which to make use of it.

1 Fry it with butter, pepper, parsley and watercress until it turns a deep golden brown on both sides. Serve it with tomatoes and mushrooms. A good sized single placenta will serve two. Check with your doctor before doing this (though be warned: he may want to share your meal!).

   WINE TIP: a rich sauterne will complement the dish.

2 A normal afterbirth contains vital minerals and semi-organic phosphates. Rose growers insist that prize blooms can be obtained if placentas are dug into the soil around the roots.

3 Remove the insides from the placenta and then preserve the outer casing in pickle. You can either stuff the placenta skin with feathers and make a small novelty cushion or you can have it converted into a re-usable ice pack by fitting a screw cap to the umbilical entry point.

Feeding your baby

There are two ways to do this – normally or by letting him suckle his mother. This second method is not to be recommended since research has shown that the following disadvantages are associated with breast feeding:

1 Your baby will grow up with a breast fetish. Girl babies who are breast fed often worry about the size and shape of their mammary glands later in life. Boy babies who are breast fed grow up to worry incessantly about the size and shape of the mammary glands of women around them.

2 The mother will be deprived of valuable natural juices and will soon look old and wizened.

3 During the period of breast feeding men will be deprived of free access to glands which nature originally designed for recreational purposes.

Inter-personal Propagation

Contraception: a subject you should know about

Here are the most important things you should remember if you want to avoid pregnancy.

1 RHYTHM METHOD

A form of contraception devised by the West Indians who couldn't afford anything else. They discovered that pregnancy rarely ensues when two people have sex while dancing. It seems that because it is difficult to keep the male organ in place contact between sperm and egg is unlikely. This form of contraception is particularly effective when used by partners of different heights.

2 THE CONTRACEPTIVE PILL

A hormone that works by reducing the female libido. Women who take the pill don't feel much like sex and so they don't get pregnant.

3 THE SHEATH

A woman who wears a tight dress will always be more difficult to impregnate.

4 THE CAP

Old fashioned headgear with a bobble on the end of a cord. Usually worn by the male partner. It makes the other partner laugh so much that intercourse is quite impossible.

5 THE CONDOM

A condom is a small apartment with thin walls. Because every noise can be heard by all the neighbours sexual activity is rare. Where a number of 'condoms' are built together the erection is known as a 'condominium'.

6 THE COIL

Funny little round thing that is placed deep inside the woman. Sperm are attracted to it because it is shiny. They swim round and round in circles, get dizzy and can either get no further or set off in the wrong direction.

7 SPERMICIDAL CREAM

Rich in fats and cholesterol, this works by giving the sperm heart attacks – bit cruel really.

8 PYJAMA TROUSERS

When worn back to front pyjama trousers make a very effective contraceptive. Widely used in Ireland. Known as a 'daddy's sauce stopper'.

9 VASECTOMY

After this operation sex is a whole different ball game. The man who has had a vasectomy doesn't ejaculate because his tubes are tied. The accumulated sperm will eventually make his testicle swell to an enormous size.

10 STANDING UP

A woman cannot get pregnant if she does it standing up.

11 THE FIRST TIME

A woman cannot get pregnant the first time she does it.

How do women get pregnant?

The fertilisation hypothesis was widely accepted for so many years that most people now find it difficult to believe that this old-fashioned theory about sperms and ova is laughably inaccurate. Belgian entomologists have now shown that conception has nothing to do with testicles, spermatozoa, ovaries or ova.

Although we know that the traditional beliefs about pregnancy are wrong, there is still considerable doubt about exactly what does happen when a woman conceives.

The following theories are the ones which seem most likely to replace the traditional 'fertilisation hypothesis'.

1   A woman can get pregnant if she opens her eyes while kissing a man.

2   A woman can get pregnant if she doesn't wash her hair on a Saturday night.

3   A woman can get pregnant if she lets a man touch her breasts on a first date.

4   A woman can get pregnant if she sits in the back row of a cinema.

Coping with a limp: things for him to say

1   It's never happened before.
2   I've been working very hard.
3   I'm sorry.
4   Is there anything else I can do for you?
5   I thought we might go out for a meal.
6   Aaaaaaaaaaaaargh.

Coping with a limp: things for her to say

1   Is it something I've done?
2   Is it something I haven't done?
3   Don't you find me attractive?

4 Don't worry. It doesn't matter.

5 It's just one of those things.

6 Call me if something comes up.

7 It's nothing.

The hazards of masturbation

Research has shown that the following disorders are associated with excessive self abuse:

1 Herpes.

2 Baldness.

3 Insanity.

4 Forgetfulness.

5 All forms of arthritis.

6 Dry skin.

7 Ingrowing toe nails.

8 Callouses on the hands.

9 Acne.

10 Something else that we can't quite remember at the moment.

How to get rid of virginity
(for women only)

1 Take up hurdling, horse riding or high jumping.

2 Join a troupe of circus acrobats.

3 Take a shorthand course.

4 Become a nurse or air stewardess.

5 Take up knitting and produce cardigans with pockets.

The F spots

In a series of staggering experiments carried out in motel rooms in Cleveland, Ohio, USA, Drs Kilroy Wasir and Vivienne ffortescue-ffortescue of the Institute of Sexual Excesses in Melbourne, Australia, succeeded in showing that women between the ages of 30 and 55 have a pair of sensitive trigger spots just behind their knee caps (the F spots).

Using tennis professionals and volunteer housewives from two nearby garden cities, Wasir and ffortescue-ffortescue showed that when these sensitive spots are stimulated for between 7 and 9 minutes the responses are undeniably sexual.

In no fewer than 89% of the women investigated, Wasir and ffortescue-ffortescue managed to raise the sexual-initiation factors by over 50% and in an astonishing 97% of the women under scrutiny they managed to lower sexual resistance by at least 75%.

According to Wasir and ffortescue-ffortescue these impressive results were obtained by training the tennis professionals to stimulate the F spots with their bare toes while pretending to discuss politics, bridge hands or grocery prices.

At first, some of the women were suspicious and resistant and the tennis professionals had to put up with a few dirty looks and withering remarks. After a few minutes, however, the resistance seemed to break down and the women began to move into positions which made it easier for their F spots to be stimulated. After an average of 8 minutes the women began to remove their clothing and by the time their F spots had been stimulated for 14 consecutive minutes all the women were desperate for sexual release.

A series of double-blind experiments (in which a team of blind tennis professionals were instructed to merely discuss politics, grocery prices and bridge hands with a matched sample of blind housewives) resulted in virtually no sexual activity, no overt signs of sexual stimulation and no observable lowering of sexual resistance.

Reproduction furniture

Obstetrician Dr Manuel Dequesteriti claims that couples wanting to start a family, or enlarge an already existing family, should enjoy intercourse in positions selected to favour conception. Since it is the depth of penetration and the length of time for which the cervical sperm lavage is allowed to remain in contact with the uterine ascent that determine the likelihood of conception, the best reproduction furniture will consist of items likely to facilitate penetration and to limit sperm dissolution.

The following items of furniture are among those considered most appropriate by Dr Dequesteriti:

1   Hospital-type bed with the mattress tilted in such a way that the feet are at least 12 inches higher than the head.

2   Zinc hip bath.

3   Chaise longue.

4   Pine kitchen table.

5   Front bench seat in a 1963 Oldsmobile.

6   Folding canvas deck chair.

7   Ejection seat in a Harrier jump jet.

Deviant forms of sexual behaviour

Professor Samuel Widge of the Institute of Sexual Studies in Moscow, Russia, claims that any form of sexual behaviour or sexual activity not practised by the majority (i.e. over 50%) of sexually active adults is 'deviant'. Using this criterion as a basis for his studies Professor Widge has now published a series of video research papers in which he has listed the ten most common forms of deviant sexual behaviour. Here is the list:

1   Removing socks before intercourse (male deviant behaviour only).

2   Removing ear-rings before intercourse (female deviant behaviour only).

3   Making love in the 'missionary' position.

4   Saying 'thank you' afterwards.

5   Bathing after intercourse.

6   Staying awake for more than 20 minutes after intercourse.

7   Falling in love.

8   Dressing entirely in cotton.

9   Not smoking a cigarette after intercourse.

10 Localised naturism (vulgarly known as 'flashing')

Pimples are a sign of sexual activity and interest

Research done in Germany has shown that people with pimples are far sexier than people without pimples. In a survey which involved 5,927 people between the ages of 14 and 76 a team of psycho-sociologists and television engineers showed that there is a direct correlation between interest in sex and the number of pimples present.

Their figures showed that:

89% of individuals with 12 or more pimples were interested in sex.

76% of individuals with 10 or 11 pimples were interested in sex.

65% of individuals with 8 or 9 pimples were interested in sex.

59% of individuals with 6 or 7 pimples were interested in sex.

45% of individuals with 4 or 5 pimples were interested in sex.

32% of individuals with 2 or 3 pimples were interested in sex.

17% of individuals with 1 pimple were interested in sex.

9% of individuals with no pimples were interested in sex.

It is not yet understood precisely why this correlation exists (observers have suggested hormonal variations, climatic variations, age differences, peer consent variability, water impurities and so on).

```
ACADEMIC MODULE FIVE

Economics, Politics,
History, Geography,
Science and
Military Studies

Advanced database for mixed students
```

A complete guide to the countries of the world

A significant common attribute among the wealthy and successful is a comprehensive knowledge of geography and the characteristics of the world's most important countries. No one can hope to understand the cut and thrust of contemporary politics or exploit the subtle variations in world trade and high finance, without knowing where places are and what happens in them. It helps a lot when you're going on holiday too, or if your plane to Stockholm is diverted to (say) Lagos.

The following information provides most of what you need to know.

Africa

Quite a large place but divided up into lots of little countries which keep fighting one another and changing their names. They grow lots of bananas and cocoa, which is pretty stupid when you consider that the whole continent is balanced on an underground treasure-trove of gold, silver, copper, diamonds, zinc, rubies, brass and all sorts of other good things.

Arabia

Large place but, like Africa, divided up into lots of little countries which keep fighting one another and changing their names. Not worth trying to keep up with them. Whole area floats on a sea of gasoline, which means that the people living there possess a lot more money than is good for them. Once the rest of the world learns how to manage without oil they'll have to get used to being poor again, which will serve them right.

Australia

Funny little island used as a stop-over for round the world sailors who need somewhere to pick up provisions. Women (all called Sheila or Matilda) spend their days sewing corks onto the rims of bush hats and selling them to tourists. Men selected for breeding are trained as dentists, anaesthetists and singers and sent to the United Kingdom or America to find wives. Not much else is known about Australia.

Canada

Big, cold and full of fir trees. No one lives there.

China

Large country about which almost nothing is known. Exports laundry workers and takeaway restaurants to the rest of the world.

France

Quite a nice little country but the people are pretty unbearable. Everyone lives in Paris from September to July, then migrates to huge Chateaux for the month of August. They all earn vast sums of money by selling apples and fiddling the Common Market. The men wear berets and corduroy trousers all the time but the women never wear anything very much, except in certain parts of Paris where they wear things so that they can take them off again. Quite good at making bread and wine but not much good at anything else.

Germany

Very efficient country where they make motor cars, fridges, machine tools and lots of other things that are too complicated to explain. The people are usually as dull as ditchwater but every now and then they get very silly and start a war. Occasionally they hold 'beer festivals' where everyone gets absolutely smashed and pretends to be French or Italian for a day or two.

Holland

Flat country entirely below sea level. Floods every time the tide comes in. Imports hippies and diamonds, exports diamonds and tulips.

Hong Kong

Important because it uses up 60% of the world's production of raw plastic. Makes funny little toys, plastic napkins, plastic cutlery, plastic bullets, plastic radios, plastic models of the Eiffel Tower, plastic dolls, plastic clothes, plastic food and plastic aeroplanes. The populace invented planned obsolescence to guarantee a working future and then discovered their lease was about to run out.

Ireland

Full of people who squabble endlessly over the Irish question, but are invariably too drunk to answer it.

Italy

Everyone wears black all the time because they're always in mourning. Men carry violin cases full of guns and shoot one another regularly. Women all have enormous breasts and gradually grow out to meet them. Government changes every week (Fridays) to give everyone an equal chance to mess things up without having to take any of the blame. Produces two sorts of wine: the stuff to drink and the stuff to flog to tourists.

Japan

Lost second world war because pilots continually flew their aeroplanes straight into enemy ships. This led to the gradual but inevitable destruction of the Japanese air force. Entire nation now dedicated to the production of cameras, television sets, pianos, motor bikes, calculators, video recorders and those funny little paper umbrellas that barmen stick into expensive cocktails. (The Japanese were the first people to produce a piano capable of speeds in excess of 100 mph.)

Liechtenstein

Richest and most powerful country in the world. There are probably only about 2,348 people living there. Rumour has it that they are all millionaires several times over. Four-fifths of the entire country is covered with brass plates announcing company regulations. Trees cost $800 a square trunk-foot to rent. 47% of the world's biggest companies have their main offices in Liechtenstein. (See also *Panama*.) The bank in Liechtenstein has a vault five times the size of Central Park.

New Zealand

Doesn't get many round the world sailors dropping in because Australia has cornered the market. Has never won the Eurovision Song Contest. Inhabited by sheep and rugby players. Probably quite a nice little country but nobody much ever goes there.

Panama

52% of the world's biggest companies have their main offices in Panama. (See *Liechtenstein*.) Has quite a lot of coast so it's not surprising that its registered shipping tonnage makes up 98% of the world's total. Exports funny hats.

Russia

Bigger and even colder than Canada. They make hammers, sickles and funny little fur hats. (But not as funny as the one made in Panama.) The women are all fat and ugly but they manage to seduce all our spies. The men are all either spies or astronauts and they can dance sitting down.

Spain

Spanish men are all waiters or bull fighters. Spanish women sit in dark rooms making lace tablecloths to sell to the tourists. A dull country; few people go there.

Switzerland

Funny little country. Should not, however, be under-estimated. If smoothed out flat would take up quite a lot of room. Never gets involved in wars. Other countries always give it their coats (and wallets) to hold. Pretends to be interested only in blowing alpine horns, yodelling, hanging bells round cows' necks, putting holes in cheese, making watches, cuckoo clocks and expensive chocolate and entertaining tourists. Is, in fact, the power behind the throne in Liechtenstein. Probably runs Panama too. Contains several lakes and funny little chalets full of gold, platinum and stock options.

United Kingdom

Still organises good social occasions (tennis tournaments, cricket matches, funerals, weddings, christenings etc). Armed forces always do well despite diet of warm beer and cold meat pies. Main exports include cricket balls, tourists and khaki shorts. Has won a war, several Nobel prizes and a Eurovision Song Contest in recent years. Provides fresh wives for Australian dentists and anaesthetists.

United States of America

Domestic scene dominated by baseball and American football (incomprehensible to outsiders) and two party political system (incomprehensible to insiders). By modern tradition world heavyweight boxing champions always come from the United States of America. Exports include cowboy films, hamburgers and cola drinks.

Understanding politics

The following glossary of political terms is designed to help the innocent observer understand what is going on in the world.

A government spokesman

Anyone who can read the PM's handwriting.

Allies

Anyone upon whom a country is financially dependent. Anyone who fought on the opposite side in a previous war.

Budget

Means of increasing overall taxation.

Communist

Someone who believes in the survival of the fittest. Communists are either very rich and powerful or else they are very weak and extremely poor.

Conservative

Anyone who owns a dark suit, drives a motor car that is less than 3 years old and has a home with fitted carpets.

Defence capacity

Capacity for attack.

Dictatorship

A method of ensuring that a single ideology is always enforced in a given country. People living in a dictatorship who disagree with the ideology in question often commit suicide by electrocution.

European Union

A group of European countries who, together with Great Britain, have volunteered to make large cash contributions to the French economy.

Extremist

Someone who holds opinions unlike one's own, or someone

who holds opinions embarrassingly like one's own.

Fascist

Someone who believes in the survival of the fittest. Fascists are either very rich and powerful or else they are very weak and extremely poor.

Liberal

Conservative democrat with fascist tendencies and sympathy for communism.

Marxist

Someone who believes in having a really good time, wearing silly moustaches, chasing girls and generally being outrageous.

Social Democrat

Someone who likes to go to lots of parties, dances, balls etc, but who also believes in equal rights, government by the people and public services paid for by someone else.

Socialist

Communist with a nice home, a car and a video recorder.

International exchange rates

With the breakdown of international monetary units imminent, the International Monetary Fellowship (IMF) has recently published a suggested 'barter' system which will have the effect of reducing inflation to zero, since all items will be equally affected. Some of the IMF's suggested barters and equivalents are outlined below.

1   One tonsillectomy = 3 week hire of a 28-foot ocean-going cabin cruiser.

2   A shampoo and set = three loaves of bread and a pint of milk.

3   A topless massage = four tins of baked beans, three boxes of cornflakes and a gallon of paraffin.

4   Repair of washing machine/TV set/any other large electrical appliance = a fortnight's holiday in Cannes, Torremolinos or Naples.

5   Repair of radio/toaster/any small electrical appliance = armful of good kindling wood and two turnips.

6   Retiling a medium sized house roof = one cwt of unpolished rice and six bottles of Australian wine.

7   Dry cleaning of one suit = four sticks of celery and half-pound pack of salt.

8   Dental extraction = one pound of dairy milk chocolates, four pound jar of boiled sweets and two large sticks of rock.

9   Golf club membership (one year) = sixty gallons of gasoline, one gallon of weedkiller and one dozen large brown eggs.

10 One hour of legal advice = Italian sports car, small diamond bracelet, flat in Monaco, thoroughbred race horse, string of polo ponies, powerboat and marina charges for six months, Cartier watch, small island off the coast of Scotland, cottage in Cornwall, modest piece of real estate in central Zurich and six pounds of new potatoes.

The ten most important figures in the history of warfare

Duke of Wellington

Before Wellington invented the boot, battles could only be fought in fine weather. The introduction of his unique footwear meant that all-weather warfare became possible. This ensured that mortality and morbidity rates could be kept at a uniform level throughout the hostilities, and this, in turn, ensured that the burial details could be kept permanently occupied instead of having to spend hours at a time with nothing to bury.

Jean Bernadotte

Bernadotte's battle victories included wins at Austerlitz and in Egypt. He campaigned in Germany and Italy and was the leading army officer throughout the period of the French Revolution. While the army figurehead Napoleon Bonaparte was messing around with Josephine it was Bernadotte who did all the tactical work. Most historians agree that the French lost at Waterloo because Bernadotte was busy having his portrait painted by Frederick Westin and Napoleon had to assume command.

Julius Caesar

Mild mannered, saucy little man who was rather vain. He wore a laurel wreath to try and disguise his premature baldness. Caesar was one of the first lawyers to go into politics – and probably one of the most successful. He survived a scandal after his liaison with an Egyptian called Cleopatra had hit the Sunday scrolls but was assassinated a few years later. Caesar's military skills were widely respected by his family and friends.

7th Earl of Cardigan

Silly man who led the charge of the Light Brigade in the Battle of Balaclava. Or rather, who should have led the charge. The weather at the time of the battle was bitter and all the soldiers were complaining of the cold. The Russians were told by their commander to knit nice little woolly helmets to keep their ears cosy but the British were ordered to knit complicated jumpers with sleeves, two pockets and four buttons. The bala-clavas didn't take as long to knit as the 'cardigans' and so the Russians were ready for battle before the British who were caught with needles in their hands instead of bayonets.

George Custer

Flamboyant US cavalry officer who'd seen so many cowboy films that he thought the cavalry always won. His false confidence led him to defeat by Sitting Bull at the Little Bighorn. Or possibly to defeat by Sitting Bighorn at Little Bull.

46

4th Earl of Sandwich

It is difficult to over-estimate the importance of the contribution to warfare of John Montague Sandwich. Before Sandwich conceived the idea of putting bits of meat and cheese between pieces of bread, soldiers either had to go hungry or spend hours laying the table in mid-battle.

George Smith Patton

Generous, gentle, self-effacing general whose modest nature made him congenitally unsuitable for a career in the armed forces. His stutter, his hesitant manner and his lack of self confidence led to his campaign tactics being marred by indecision. Later in his career he chose to work not as a fighting man but as a hospital orderly where he could offer sympathy and understanding to the injured troops.

T.E. Lawrence

Soldier who got on very well with the Arabs – particularly the younger ones with long silky eyelashes. Later wrote some rather dirty books about coal miners in central England.

King Arthur

Led a group of middle class do-gooders called the Knights of the Round Table who spent their days wandering around the countryside killing dragons, rescuing damsels in distress and galloping over freshly sown cornfields. Arthur's wife had a rumbustious affair with one of the Knights (called Lancelot) and Arthur threw her out. With no wife to look after him Arthur had to do all his own cooking and this led to his downfall. He was burnt to death while trying to put out a fire which had started when he was baking some cakes.

Hannibal

Commander in Chief of the Carthiginian army at the tender age of 26. Hannibal's main problem was that he had very expensive tastes. To pay for his many mistresses and to enable him to keep a bar-bill in double figures, Hannibal started smuggling elephants across the Alps into Southern Gaul where he sold them to circuses. Chased by customs officers, he wandered around Europe for several years but finally, facing a court martial and inevitable disgrace, poisoned himself.

The most important figures in the history of science

Archimedes

One of the cleanest scientists who ever lived. Archimedes spent much of his time trying to work out why bath water always goes down the plug-hole in the same way. He had all sorts of different bath tubs made but the water always left in a clockwise direction. He never solved the problem but went mad after emigrating to Australia.

Ivan Petrovich Pavlov

Pavlov is remembered as the scientist who showed that dogs can be trained to salivate when they hear a dinner bell. (This wasn't news, of course, but everyone pretended that it was because there hadn't been a famous Russian scientist for centuries and people felt sorry for them.) What isn't known anywhere near as well, is that the great man was, in fact, only doing what he had been trained to do. When he was a student at St Petersburg, the young Pavlov was subjected to a subliminal indoctrination programme and his research studies were a response to suggestions made by Professor Ryazan.

Albert Einstein

Einstein succeeded in producing a formula so complicated that no one could tell whether it was a hoax or a useful piece of scientific work. Because he had long white hair and always wore open toed sandals he was given the benefit of the doubt, a post at an American university and a Nobel Prize.

Galileo

Italian scientist who got into dreadful trouble with the authorities because of his dangerous habit of dropping stones over the edge of the Leaning Tower of Pisa. Twelve citizens were killed in one week alone thanks to this madman's experiments and eventually he had to be locked up.

Isaac Newton

Newton's work on apples and apple trees did much to revolutionise a flagging European fruit industry. It was Newton who discovered that apples fall off trees if they aren't picked.

Alexander Graham Bell

Bell had a miserable childhood because of his name. Other schoolboys used to tease him and run after him yelling 'Brrr Brrr' and 'Ring Ring'. Bell got so depressed by all this that he swore he would get his own back. When he grew up he invented the telephone and made everyone else's life as miserable as his own had been.

Thomas Edison

Prolific inventor who gave us the electric lamp, the record player, the radio, the television set, the toaster, the electric toothbrush, the film projector, the electric cooker, the video recorder, the electric typewriter, the cassette recorder, the blender, the electric car window, the electric floor polisher, the street lamp, the automatic wind-on camera, the electronic game, the washing machine, the deep freeze, the electric kettle, the refrigerator, the automatic coffee grinder, the percolator, the electric eel, the car windscreen wipers, the electric organ and the electrocardiogram.

ACADEMIC MODULE SIX

Recreational Calisthenics

Sport, fitness and exercises
- Compulsory -

Safety guidelines for observers

Research has shown that many people make the grave mistake of thinking that watching sport is a safe activity and can be enjoyed without any professional preparation. They are wrong. Many reports have detailed the hazards involved in amateur spectatorship and the evidence is now substantial. A committee of leading American recreologists from the University of Maine has shown that 64.7% of all deaths involving American males in their third decade occur before, during or after the watching of physical exercise. In Britain, researchers at the Twickenham Institute of Sport Observation have shown that 98% of all adult males who die before the age of fifty have spent some time watching sport. In France Dr H. Jérome Farr, who has an international doctorate in sport philosophy from the University of Versailles, claims that the links between sport spectating and disease are now so well established that anyone who ignores the dangers and watches sport without proper preparation is lacking essential diligence in the matter of health.

Dr Farr argues that the spectators most at risk are those tempted to watch cup finals, tennis championships, golf competitions and so on without proper pre-tournament preparation.

'It's like trying to run a mile in under four minutes without any training,' he complains sadly.

To aid all would-be spectators, we have compiled a set of training notes:

1   Before beginning any programme of spectatorship you must be certain that your health is suitable. Weak eyes can lead to strain, throat ailments can be seriously aggravated by enthusiastic appreciation, and cardiac conditions which may not be immediately apparent, can be worsened by watching violent exercise.

2   Begin by watching TV sports programmes in very short bursts. If you haven't spectated before you should start by experiencing sound or vision alone. Choose a dull match and watch it on your video recorder. Make sure that you know the final result before you start watching. Uncertainty can add to the hazards associated with spectatorship.

3   In the early stages of your spectating career, watch televised sports that you do not like and do not understand. Show jumping, lacrosse, ice skating and cross country embroidery are just four of the lesser known sports which seem particularly suitable for beginners.

4   Watch a video recording of old weather forecasts. If you feel excited switch off immediately.

5   Once you can watch a 60 minute programme devoted to a sport you neither like nor understand, you can expose yourself to a 10 minute collection of low-lights from a sport you do find attractive. Again, make sure that you know the result of the match you choose to watch. Do not watch a match involving any team or individual you might be tempted to support.

6   If you intend to watch 'live' sport at some time in the future, you should begin now to prepare yourself for all the accompanying stresses. Turn your television set so that it faces a window and then put a chair outside in a position where you can watch the screen. Sit down on your chair at least 90

minutes before the programme is due to start. Make sure that all doors to your home are locked so that you cannot make hot drinks or use the plumbing facilities. When the programme you have chosen to watch is finished, wait outside for another 90 minutes before letting yourself back into the house.

7   After practising outside your own home for three months, you should be ready to try out your skill at 'live' spectating. Start by attending a gentle sport such as snooker, darts, bowls or chess, then gradually work your way up to athletics, basket ball and tennis. Finally, if all goes well, you can buy tickets to watch motor-car racing, football or underwater trampolining.

8   Get in plenty of practice at local 'amateur' sports meetings. Find out when local clubs are holding tournaments and attend as many of those as you can. Watch other people's children competing and you'll quickly build up the sort of resilience you'll need if you intend to watch big time professional sports stars.

9   After allowing this sort of regime for a few months you'll be ready to buy yourself a ticket for a major golf tournament, an ice hockey match or an international archery contest.

10 Build up slowly and you should find spectating a fairly safe occupation. Most very fit people can accommodate high level spectating within 6 to 12 months of starting. It is, however, important to avoid excessive enthusiasm for the first two years.

Psychotherapeutic isometric exercises

Some people think that to get fit you have to run around and get sweaty. Perhaps they're the kind of enthusiasts who take up circuit training. They run for two hundred yards, they do twenty press ups, they jog for half a mile, they juggle with two medicine balls for sixty seconds, they skip for four hundred yards and they vomit for two minutes. All this is dangerous and silly, especially when there's a relatively safe method of achieving fitness without any sort of exertion at all. For years, doctors have understood the dramatic effect the brain can have on the body and the immense value of self-hypnotic techniques. If you imagine you're taking exercise – and if your imagination is sufficiently strong – then the benefits to your physique will soon become apparent.

This sort of sweat-free activity is called psychotherapeutic isometric exercise (PIE). You should begin the exercises in this programme by selecting the simplest and least painful routines. As with traditional 'active' exercise, if you do too much too soon you'll risk damaging your musculature.

The PIE Programme

1   Imagine that you are taking the top off your pen. Feel the muscles in your hand tighten as you seize the cap. Imagine that your tendons strain as they meet the resistance. Close your eyes tightly and feel the muscles in your chest hardening as the effort increases. Finally, allow yourself a moment or two of relaxation as the pen top comes away from the body of the pen.

2   Imagine that you are winking. (If you are an occidental you should take extra care with this exercise. Orientals can perform psychotherapeutic isometric winking without too much effort because their lid-travel distance is minimal.) Once your first wink is complete, rest for 30 seconds. Breathe deeply and slowly. Then imagine another wink. Limit yourself to 12 imaginary winks for your first session. Later you may be able to build up to 20 or 30 imaginary winks. Some experts can even manage forty winks.

3   Imagine that you are wiggling your toes. Wiggle just one or two to start with. Then rest them. Then imagine that you are wiggling all the toes on one foot. After a long rest, imagine that you are wiggling all the toes on both feet. Do not try this exercise if you are taking any prescribed medication.

4   Imagine that you are riding an exercise bike. Be sure to imagine a light if you are riding at night. Imagine the bedroom floor vibrating and the noise of the pedals going round. If you find this exercise too easy, imagine that you are riding an exercise bike under water!

5   Imagine that you are weight lifting. Start with quite small weights. Then gradually increase your concentration until you are lifting quite big weights. Feel your muscles strain and your body heave as you get those weights off the ground. Feel your hernia grow as the session continues.

The secret of anaerobic exercise

In anaerobic exercise the aim is to deprive the body of oxygen for as long a period as possible. Without oxygen the body must concentrate its existing resources and thereby improve its exercise capabilities. The lungs become more efficient at extracting every last molecule of oxygen from the air within them. The blood circulates more slowly. The liver expands three times its normal size in order to ensure that its physiological functions are maintained. The brain shuts down unnecessary lobes and concentrates on survival and full sexual function. Unnecessary parts of the body such as the kidneys, the feet and the ear lobes are deprived of oxygen while vital organs in the groin area receive an undiminished supply.

Looking after your dentures: passive exercise for greater strength

Until the University of Schaffhausen installed a Chair of Denture Care, denture science had been an unheralded, almost forgotten backwater of medical endeavour. Now that the Swiss have led the way, however, scientists around the globe are beginning to take this subject far more seriously.

If you are one of the world's 3,679 million registered denture wearers, then you too can benefit from this simple denture-strengthening exercise.

1   Take out your dentures.

2   Place them on a clean, smooth, flat surface.

3   Hold the dentures in position with your left hand and with your right hand pick up a piece of fruit – a pear or an apple, for example.

4   Rub the piece of fruit against the dentures. Rub as hard as you can until the fruit has been torn into tiny pieces.

5   You must do this simple, preliminary, strengthening exercise once a day for seven days.

6   For advanced strengthening exercises you need a piece of treacle toffee. Hold the dentures in position with your left hand. Rub the toffee against the dentures with your right hand. Toffee is much tougher than fruit so you will need to rub harder.

7   Follow this advanced exercise once a day for another seven days and your dentures will be stronger and more capable of dealing with tough foodstuffs.

Understanding sport: the official rules of some of the world's most important sports and games

Archery

1   The standard target shall be:

(a) a wand made of willow, or

(b) a straw facsimile of the sheriff of Nottingham, or

(c) an apple not less than 150 gm in weight and not more than 250 gm in weight.

2   The archer shall be provided with equipment which shall consist of a bow, a bow string, a bowsight, a bowmark, a finger protector, a quiver full of arrows and a funny little green hat.

3   The archer shall be dressed in a green nylon leotard, a green lightweight, washable jerkin, thigh length brown suede boots and a simulated leather waistcoat decorated with four little pockets and fastened with three leather covered buttons. Advertising material must not be worn.

4   The archer shall aim at the target from a distance of 200 paces.

5   The Lady Paramount shall be the supreme arbitrator on all matters connected with the Tournament. The Lady Paramount shall always be a beautiful virgin and shall, where possible, be of royal lineage.

6   The prize shall always be a silver arrow.

Croquet

1   The standard court shall be a rectangle measuring 35 yards by 28 yards. The four corners shall be known as Corner 1, Corner 2, Corner 3 and Corner 4. The sides of an inner rectangle parallel to and one yard within the outer rectangle shall be known as the one yard lines. Balls resting on the corner spots shall be known as 'corner balls'. Balls resting on the one yard line shall be known as the 'one yard balls'.

2   The equipment shall consist of:

(a) The hoops. Made of iron, aluminium or molybdenum the hoops shall be painted white. The sides of the hoops shall be 3½ inches apart.

(b) The balls. The balls shall be coloured blue, red, black and yellow. The blue coloured ball shall be known as the 'blue ball'. The red coloured ball shall be known as the 'red ball'. The black coloured ball shall be known as the 'black ball'. The yellow coloured ball shall be known as the 'yellow ball'. The balls shall be 3¾ inches in diameter.

(c) The peg. The peg shall be made of wood and painted in pretty colours.

(d) The mallets. The mallets shall be made of wood and shall be used for knocking the hoops and peg into the ground.

3   Balls not on the court shall be known as balls off the court.

4   Players shall have turns alternately.

5   The aim of the game is to hit your own balls through the hoops and to hit the vicar's balls out of court.

Netball

1   The court shall have a smooth, firm surface.

2   The ball shall be a netball.

3   There shall be a goal post at each end of the court. There may, or may not, be a piece of netting attached to the metal ring at the top of each goal post.

4   The aim of the game is to toss or throw the netball through the metal ring at the top of each goal post.

5   There shall be seven players on each side. Each team shall defend one goal post and attack the other.

6   All players shall be female. No player shall be more than 22 years of age nor less than 16 years of age. Players shall be not more than 5 ft 8 ins tall and not less than 5 ft 2 ins tall; they shall weigh not more than 150 pounds and not less than 112 pounds. The individual measurements of the players shall be as follows:

(a) hips: no more than 39 ins and no less than 34 ins

(b) waist: no more than 32 ins and no less than 22 ins

(c) bust: no more than 46 ins and no less than 34 ins.

7   At the start of each match the players shall tuck their skirts or dresses into their knickers.

8   Every time a goal is scored the players shall jump up and down and kiss one another. Players with bust sizes in excess of 38ins shall not jump up and down but may kiss one another.

Tug of war

1 Teams shall consist of men, women or a mixture of men and women.

2 All players shall be alive at the start of the contest.

3 All players shall wear clothing, particularly if the weather is cold.

4 The equipment shall consist of a piece of rope. It will be a long piece of rope. And quite thick.

5 One team will hold onto the end of the rope.

6 The other team will hold onto the other end of the rope.

7 The two teams will face each other and pull in opposing directions.

8 When the rope breaks the team with the longest piece of rope shall have a wish.

Water polo

1 The field of play should not be wider than 20m and not longer than 30m. Clear markings, made on the surface of the water with white paint, should show the goal lines, the half distance lines, the four metre lines, the two metre lines and all other lines.

2 The water shall not be colder than 50 deg F and not hotter than 70 deg F at any time during the match.

3 One team must wear dark blue caps and the other team must wear white caps. Players must also wear swimming costumes. If a woman player accidentally loses part or all of her costume then play shall stop until such time as she has recovered her costume and her composure. If a man player accidentally loses his costume then the loss shall be deemed to be deliberate and the player shall be excluded from the game.

4 If one player should foul another player then the referee shall award a free throw.

5   If a player should foul the water then the match shall be abandoned.

6   Splashing is not allowed.

7   If a player accidentally drowns during the match then his team shall be allowed to introduce a substitute. If a player is deliberately drowned by a member of the opposing team, a substitute shall be allowed and a free throw awarded.

Radical Philology and Dialectology

Advanced modern languages course

Understanding English

Many people use language in a confusing and imprecise way. In an attempt to avoid some of the problems which can ensue, the American Board of Statistical Analysis has studied a random sample of 37% of North American word-users. From the material they accumulated, the Board succeeded in defining some of the words most people commonly used in an unscientific way.

The American Board of Statistical Analysis estimated that 13.6% of American schools, colleges and businesses have already accepted the new definitions, which are printed below as a public service.

Never = 2.3% of the time
Rarely = 4.8% of the time
Exceptionally = 5.7% of the time
Infrequently = 11% of the time
Occasionally = 14% of the time
Sometimes = 45% of the time
A lot = 49% of the time
Normally = 50% of the time
Not infrequently = 51% of the time

More often than not = 53.9% of the time
Usually = 59% of the time
Often = 60.1% of the time
Commonly = 62.4% of the time
Frequently = 67% of the time
Almost always = 78% of the time
Always = 97% of the time
For ever = 98.8% of the time

How to decide what people really mean

Like body language, clichés are a part of the way in which we communicate with one another. Saying precisely what you mean is really as rude as staring or pointing and the cliche offers a means of euphemistic expression that relieves us of the need for painful plain-speaking. Here are some of the most commonly used clichés, together with their interpretations.

'It'll do you good' REALLY MEANS: 'It'll do me good'.

'Don't you think it would be a good idea if...' REALLY MEANS: 'I think it would be a good idea if...'

'I like your hair that way' REALLY MEANS: 'It hides more of your face'.

'You're looking very well' REALLY MEANS: 'My God, you've put on a lot of weight'.

'It suits you' REALLY MEANS: 'We shut in two minutes and I've got a date tonight with a gorgeous bloke who rattled my fillings last Saturday night. Besides, we've had that in stock for three months now and it'll have to go into the sale if you don't buy it'.

'It's for your own good' REALLY MEANS: 'I want you to'.

'We have a lot in common' REALLY MEANS: 'I used to go out with your wife'.

'Don't give it another thought' REALLY MEANS: 'I'll never forgive you'.

'It really doesn't matter' REALLY MEANS: 'It matters'.

'This will hurt' REALLY MEANS: 'This will hurt'.

'With all due respect' REALLY MEANS: 'I despise you'.

'Honestly…' REALLY MEANS: 'This isn't true, but you might just believe it'.

'It's only a little prick' REALLY MEANS: 'I'm sorry'.

'I love you' REALLY MEANS: 'I want to go to bed with you'.

'This won't hurt' REALLY MEANS: 'This will hurt'.

'Do you love me?' REALLY MEANS: 'I want to go to bed with you'.

'You are clever' REALLY MEANS: 'I want some of your money'.

'It's on my desk right now' REALLY MEANS: 'I've lost it'.

'I've never seen anything like it' REALLY MEANS: 'Ugh'.

'It's what he would have wanted' REALLY MEANS: 'It's what I want'.

'Your hands are cold' REALLY MEANS: 'Your hands are cold'.

'Some of my best friends are…' REALLY MEANS: 'I'm not really the bigot you think I am. And even if I am why shouldn't I be?'

'You're right at the top of the list' REALLY MEANS: 'You're equal first with 278,495 other people'.

'It's the only answer' REALLY MEANS: 'It's the only answer I'm prepared to accept'.

'Please be reasonable' REALLY MEANS: 'Do as you're told'.

'Pull yourself together' REALLY MEANS: 'You look a mess and I hate scenes'.

'You're making a fool of yourself' REALLY MEANS: 'You're embarrassing me'.

'There's a lot of it about' REALLY MEANS: 'I don't know what it is'.

'You'll get over it' REALLY MEANS: 'I've already got over it'.

'You are safe aren't you?' REALLY MEANS: 'I'm coming'.

Collective nouns and collective thinking

Everyone knows that a collection of fish is a shoal, a group of birds a flock, and that geese, dogs, horses and cattle are collectively known as a gaggle, a pack, a string and a herd.

If you've ever been confused about how to describe groups of people then learn this list. Your friends will be most impressed.

A hamper of assistants
A congregation of clergymen
A galaxy of actresses
A pride of expectant fathers
A knot of scouts
A shower of weather forecasters
A swarm of heating engineers
A congestion of children
A clump of labourers
A drove of chauffeurs
A clutch of car mechanics
A wealth of publishers
A collection of philatelists
A press of laundry workers
A ring of proctologists
A batch of cooks
A stream of urologists
A tuft of trichologists
A quantity of surveyors
A pack of postmen
A band of rubber workers
A cast of sculptors
A cluster of diamond cutters
A ring of jewellers
A posse of vets
A bunch of florists
A nest of mothers
A stack of booksellers / librarians
A lot of auctioneers
A corps of pathologists

A congress of prostitutes
A concentration of students
A body of undertakers
A company of representatives
A set of osteopaths
A dossier of policemen
A sheaf of administrators
A pile of gastroenterologists
An aggregation of biochemists
An association of psychologists
A drift of skiers
A clutch of physiotherapists
A school of nurses
A meeting of social workers
A herd of audiologists
A convergence of opticians
An issue of journalists
A brood of midwives
A community of public health officials
A cell of cytologists
A branch of foresters
A line of geneticists
A chain of chemists
A growth of endocrinologists
A cloud of spiritualists
A catch of obstetricians
A mass of oncologists
A smear of laboratory technicians
A promenade of chiropodists
A gathering of dress makers
A camaraderie of photographers
A host of bacteriologists
An order of waiters
A pyramid of archaeologists
A race of anthropologists
A giggle of teenage girls
A hold of sailors

A grip of luggage handlers
A slump of economists
A grievance of defendants
A whinge of consumers
A bore of mining engineers
A nerd of computer specialists
A bosom of typists

How to speak foreign languages

Some people spend many days and a small fortune learning how to speak foreign languages fluently. It is, however, quite possible to get on well with foreigners simply by learning the rudiments of their languages.

French

Facial expressions play an important part. You must learn to open your eyes really wide, to purse your lips, to blow out your cheeks and to hold your head on one side as though you had a stiff neck. Despite protestations made by elderly academics, French is more a regional variation of English than a language of its own right and you won't have any problems making yourself understood if you say things like 'hamburger', 'weekend', 'picnic', 'cul-de-sac', 'café', and 'cognac' as though you were trying to imitate Maurice Chevalier.

Italian

Very easy language. Add an 'o' and 'i' to everything and wave your arms about a lot. Shout if people don't understand you.

Japanese

There are only five basic words in Japanese. These are 'yen', 'Honda', 'Yamaha', 'Sony', and 'Sayonara'. When talking Japanese it is important to keep your teeth tightly clenched and to screw up your eyes. Mutter the five basic words in any order you like and take lots of photographs of the person you are talking to.

German

All German words need to be formed in the back of the throat. They should be spat out as though they were slightly distasteful. Use plenty of spittle and keep your mouth well moistened. The Germans also have a funny habit of runningalltheirwordstogetherlikethissothattheyproduceimmenselydifficultlookingwordswithouttoomucheffortatall. This technique was a form of encoding formulated early this century when Germany was given to attacking smaller and weaker countries without warning. The habit has remained. To speak German fluently you need to stab your finger in the air a lot and to add -ch to just about everything.

Spanish

A bit like Italian but talk quietly and don't wave your arms about quite as much.

Chinese

Very easy language to master. The basic principle is that you must miss out every other word in a sentence. You must also avoid using the letter 'r' in those words which normally contain it, putting it instead into those words which normally contain an 'l'. So, for example, 'rice' becomes 'lice' in Chinese, while 'lady' becomes 'rady'. You'll find this confusing until you get used to it because some words take on an entirely different meaning. So, a 'crutch' is something used for changing gear in a motor car while a 'clutch' is a genital area. Try to nod your head backwards and forwards a good deal while speaking Chinese.

Welsh

Easiest language of all because although lots of people pretend to speak it no one really does. The secret is to allow your vocal pitch to fluctuate a good deal. Look very serious because no one ever smiles when speaking Welsh. This is partly because there aren't any Welsh jokes and partly because the sort of people who pretend to speak Welsh don't have much of a sense of humour.

Practical Mechanical Engineering

An essential course for beginners

Motor car maintenance

No course of this sort would be complete without information on the most vital piece of twentieth-century equipment – the motor car. It is essential to remove and clean the engine every 3,000 miles. If you fail to do this grease, oil, road dirt and other debris can adversely affect the performance of your car. The instructions given below apply to all models.

PROCEDURE

Locate the carburettor piston flange casing and loosen the four deep-set screw washers in the outer fulcrum joints. Be careful to make sure that you do not dislodge the exhaust feed pipe as you do this. Next, use a cobalt ball socket faucet wrench to unfasten the eight settling rockers on the forward engine mounting. Undo the four cam tampets which operate the hydraulic push rod and loosen the chain tensioning sprocket which connects the crankshaft to the sliding block. Unline the cylinders so that you can unfasten the connecting rods in the centres of each of the universal half shafts. To avoid damaging the valve seats make sure that when you ream the combustion space centre point you don't trap the double hairpin springs in the oil gasket. Remove the valve gear pistons and bearing shells by unfastening the gudgeon pins. Flex the clutch hosing and empty the radiator before you syphon the contents of the sealed filler cap basin.

You should now find that your engine can be lifted out of the engine compartment. You may need someone to help you with this.

Once the engine has been taken out of its housing you must unfasten all the house brackets, bolt separators and nut controls. When this has been done you will find that the engine will quickly fall into all its component parts. There should be somewhere between 187 and 45,920 separate parts according to the complexity of your engine.

Each part should then be washed individually in warm, soapy water. When the parts have been thoroughly washed and all traces of oil and grease have been removed they should be rinsed in cold water. Dry the parts carefully with an old towel but do make sure that you do not leave small strands of cloth adhering to the metal.

Leave the engine parts to air overnight and reassemble within twenty-four hours.

Servicing your heart-lung machine and home defibrillator

(Important: first make sure that no one is using the heart-lung machine or defibrillator. Also check that no one is likely to need the machines for at least two hours.)

Begin by unfastening the operating brackets and disconnecting the discharge capacitor. You'll see that the oscillator and control components can easily be disengaged from the solid state synthesising circuitry. Once you've done this you will be able to free the cardiac electrodes and measure the falling electrostatic charge on your joule meter. Allow the stored energy to trickle into a secure non-porous container.

Check the vacuum in the voltage selector and make sure that

the aluminium chassis is nicely polished. The waveform changing choke and haemoglobinometer will need de-stimulating and you'll also have to check the pulsing of the high input resistance oxygen injection moulding.

Finally, give the stainless steel housing a good rub over with an oily rag.

ACADEMIC MODULE NINE

Advanced Jurisprudence

Complete law studies

How to practise law

1 Think of a big number. Add a couple of noughts to it.
2 Show the number to your secretary.
3 Get her to write the number on a bill – and to send it to your client.
4 Bank the cheque.
5 Buy a big new house.
6 Use any leftover money to buy another Ferrari.
7 Go back to 1.

Bipedal Therapeutics (autocontrol)

First aid course

How to make your medicine cabinet

Making a medicine cabinet isn't difficult. Almost anyone can do it. To start with you need six pieces of wood. The pieces should all be the same size. It might be sensible to find pieces that are 2 feet square. This will save you the bother of worrying about whether or not you've got the right piece of wood and whether or not it's the right way up.

Begin by putting one piece of wood flat on the floor. This will be the base of your medicine cabinet. Now hold a second piece of wood above the first, so that it is two feet up in the air and parallel to the first piece of wood. This will be the roof of your medicine cabinet. To keep the roof of your medicine cabinet where it is now, you're going to have to put in some walls.

To make your first wall take a third piece of wood and hold it vertically so that it connects the base of your medicine cabinet with the roof. Since it is going to be a wall this third piece of wood should be placed right at the edge of the base and the roof.

Now, hold the roof and the wall in position with one hand

and pick up a nail and a hammer with your other hand. Hammer the nail in so that the wall and roof are firmly fixed together.

The next thing you have to do is nail the wall to the base of the medicine cabinet. If you didn't have a proper plan to follow this could be very difficult indeed. However, there is a trick that skilled carpenters use and you can use it too. It is really remarkably simple!

Turn the roof and the wall upside down so that your roof temporarily becomes the base of your medicine cabinet.

Now, you can nail the base to the wall by pretending that it is the roof. It isn't the roof, of course. It is really still the base. But since you're going to turn the whole thing over again very soon the deception will not hurt anyone. Most people will probably never know what you've done. This really will make your work much easier.

Now that you've got the roof and the base of your medicine cabinet connected by one wall you're ready to add some more walls. This isn't too difficult. Just pick up your fourth and fifth pieces of wood and nail them to the sides of your cabinet at top and bottom. Make sure that these two new sides are in contact with the rear wall. The front wall of the cabinet is going to be the door so don't add that yet!

Before you add the door to your cabinet you must put the whole structure into position. Pick a spot in your bathroom that is relatively free of wires and pipes and get everyone in the family to agree that the position you've selected is the right one. Now pick up your medicine cabinet. It probably looks a bit like a box on its side! Hold the cabinet against the wall with its own back wall in close contact with whatever is on the inside of the bathroom wall.

Before nailing the cabinet to the wall, do make sure that it is level. Put an apple or an orange on top of the cabinet and move the cabinet around until the piece of fruit seems to be stable. If you haven't got an apple or an orange a tennis ball will do. It will certainly be better than a banana. In fact a banana won't be much use at all.

Once you're happy about the position of your cabinet, nail the back wall to the bathroom wall. Use big, strong nails and hit them very hard.

Now that the cabinet is fixed to the bathroom wall you can put the door on. Place the final piece of wood against the opening of your cabinet and gently tap some nails into the edges. These will hold the door in position. It is extremely important that you do *not* hammer the nails all the way in. You will need to be able to open the door to your cabinet if you are going to put things in and take them out again. In preparation for this, hammer one more nail into the bathroom wall. Use one of your strong masonry nails and hammer it in as high as you can reach.

This nail will hold a pair of pincers and your hammer. When you want to take something out of the cabinet, pull out the door-nails with the pincers. Then, when you have finished, you can close the cabinet by using the hammer to re-insert the nails.

Putting a shelf in is optional; and complicated.

Stocking your medicine cabinet

Once you've made your medicine cabinet you'll want to know what to put in it. We sent questionnaires to 14,000 people in England, Germany, America, France, Australia and Gibraltar asking them what sort of things they kept in their cabinets. With the aid of the results we obtained we have prepared a list of the most popular items.

Small, half empty bottles of aspirins. Most of the tablets should have turned brown.

Half empty, brown bottle with no label. The contents should be murky in colour.

Small, completely empty tube of pile-ointment, without cap.

Empty tampon box with special offer printed on the side.

White plastic container in which there are 3 Valium tablets.

Sticking plaster tin containing two rusty razor blades.

A black comb.
Three small screws and a handful of assorted washers.
1 pair of nail scissors.
Toothbrush with splayed bristles.

Home surgery made simple

NOTE: *This advice is suitable only for bald left-handed former nuclear scientists aged 120 or more.*

Waiting lists for operations are often long and surgeons' fees can be very high. You can overcome both problems by learning how to perform surgery on yourself. Of course, you have to remember that some operations are far too complicated for the beginner. Even quite gifted amateurs will have difficulty in coping with delicate neurosurgical procedures. Amputations can be pretty tricky too.

Before you do anything at all you must plan your operation. You may have a cool nerve, steady hands and an incisive mind but you won't get far without a few instruments. Planning is all important in surgery. There is nothing worse than getting to the end of an operation and discovering that you don't have anything with which to close the wound. You'll find that a walk to the local surgical appliances shop is twice as long when you're having to hold the edges of a gaping wound together. Remember how it feels when there isn't any toilet paper left? Well, it'll be a lot worse than that!

The first decision you must make concerns the nature of the operation you intend to perform. Here are some of the operations you can choose from: tonsillectomy, hip replacement, orchidopexy, mammaplasty and hemicolectomy. There are lots of other operations; some of them difficult to pronounce and some of them quite impossible to spell. Don't allow yourself to drift into doing an operation just because you can pronounce it. Try and choose one that will be useful. I suggest that you try an exploratory laparotomy or a simple cholecystectomy to start with since the mortality rates associated with these two operations are relatively slight.

Having decided on an operation you must next collect together all the instruments and equipment you're likely to need. A good basic kit will include: foot operated suction pump, biactive hyfrecator, platinum tipped cautery burner, heavy duty gynaecological transformer, proctosigmoid desiccation set, universal needle set, angle ball electrode, Babinski's percussor, diathermy scalpel handle, Halsted's 'misquito' artery forceps, Blackhaus' towel clips, Lister's sinus forceps, Forester's sponge holding forceps, Littauer stisch scissors, Wright's needle holder, Crile Murray's needle holder, aural syringe, McKay nail elevator, seamless aluminium ear trough, Jobson Horne probe, Formby cerumen scoop and hook, Thudichum's nasal specula, Higgonson's rubber syringe, Rose's sinus douching cannula, post nasal and laryngeal atomizer, St Clair Thomson's rhinoscopic mirrors, Naunton Morgan's rectal speculum, universal lighting attachment, Barron haemorrhoidal ligator, dissecting forceps, uterine curette, Horrock's uterine sound, heavy duty cautery outfit, Macrae mucous extractor, umbilical dilator, Portex umbilical cannula, disposable surgical gloves, self healing bisexual urinal.

You'll also need a large cardboard box filled with assorted syringes, needles, towels and paper tissues. You won't need to bother with a mask. Surgeons only wear masks so that they won't be recognised afterwards.

Most of the instruments I've described can be obtained from any surgical supply store but if you have difficulty in finding some of them try approaching your local hospital. Offer to buy or rent an armful of assorted instruments. You will need at least an armful for any useful operation.

Having chosen an operation and having collected a bundle of instruments, you must next decide on the best site. You can, of course, perform your operation just about anywhere but it might prove sensible to opt for the kitchen. For one thing there will probably be a large table there. What's more, the floor and walls will probably be fairly easy to clean. If your home is equipped with a specially furnished operating theatre then there will, of course, be no problem.

Next you must have a good shave. Not just the hair on your face; you must shave your entire body. Little germs and other nasty things can hide among the hairs – particularly the tightly packed curly ones – and so it is vitally important to remove every last millimetre of stubble.

Finally, before you start it's wise to take the telephone off the hook and put any animals in another room. You don't want people ringing up when you're half way through a liver transplant to ask you round for coffee; nor do you want your dog to hang about begging for scraps. It might be a good idea to lock and bolt the back door too. Neighbours and tradesmen who might wander in by mistake may bring fresh germs with them. They are very unlikely to have shaved off all their hair before coming to see you.

With everything ready you can now begin. Pull the table into a good position where the light is evenly distributed. Put a pillow or a pile of towels under your head so that you can see what you're doing. Unfasten your skirt or your trousers and part your clothing so that you can see the whole area involved. If you are going to perform brain surgery you can keep all your clothes on.

Before you cut through the skin you must give yourself an anaesthetic, of course. This is really quite important. I suggest that you turn on the television and watch for twenty minutes. Do not watch any programme for longer than this: you mustn't render yourself completely unconscious, or you'll have difficulty in continuing with the actual procedure. You can start cutting just as soon as you begin to feel woozy.

If, for example, you have decided to perform a gall bladder removal operation on yourself, you can now set to work in search of the gall bladder. The following outline will demonstrate how simple it all is.

You will, of course, have unfastened your trousers (or skirt) and pulled your shirt (or blouse) right up under your chin. (You may even like to remove your clothing altogether. Do remember to draw the kitchen curtains if you do this.) Your gall bladder is nestling somewhere under your right ribs and that is where you are going to be working.

The first cut must take you right to the site, so it is important to make it in the correct place. Don't make half a dozen cuts or you're going to find sewing up again afterwards a real nightmare. The cut should be precisely situated under those ribs of yours. Do make a good deep cut and don't be tempted to mess around with a lot of wimpish little nicks. A really sharp slash with your scalpel will take you straight through the skin, the subcutaneous fat, the fasia, the muscle layers and the peritoneum. Poke your hand through the hole you've made and feel around inside. Once you've found the gall bladder (and you can't fail to recognise it) you can use your scissors to cut it away from the other internal tissues. There may be a little bleeding but there shouldn't be anything that a stypic pencil won't stop. (A stypic pencil, by the way, is a very useful surgical item.)

With the gall bladder out of the way, all that remains is to sew up the wound again. That shouldn't take more than a minute or two. It really is an extremely simple business and it's astonishing to think that surgeons make so much of a fuss about it.

Give yourself five minutes to recover and then get up off the table and make yourself a nice cup of tea. (That is another advantage of operating in the kitchen – the kettle isn't far away.) Don't forget to throw your gall bladder away. Wrap it in a paper bag if you're going to put it into the dustbin. As you relax with your tea, you can reflect smugly on the huge amounts of time and money you've saved.

Do-it-yourself acupuncture

NOTE: *This advice is only suitable for three-legged foetuses.*

Acupuncture is a simple, effective, cheap and painless way to deal with pain, fever, arthritis, obesity, deafness, myopia, impotence, premature ejaculation, pregnancy, cancer, infertility, tuberculosis, hypermetropia, ingrowing toe nails, dry skin, dandruff, myxodema, wet skin, acne, piles, appendicitis, varicose veins, gastritis, pneumonia, angina, high blood pressure, greenfly, low blood pressure, malaria, bankruptcy, phlebitis, sleeping sickness, warts, insomnia, moles, badgers, splits ends and all disorders that begin with the letter 'F'.

Because skilled acupuncturists are often difficult to find we have devised a simple form of do-it-yourself acupuncture. To gain the benefits described above simply follow these instructions:

1   Find a needle of some sort. Gramophone, knitting, sewing or surgical will do.

2   Commission a local printer to produce an impressive looking diploma. It doesn't have to say anything particular but it must be composed in ideograms (funny-looking Chinese writing).

3   Start putting letters after your name. It doesn't really matter what letters you choose but remember that more than three letters look ostentatious. (Less than three looks tawdry.)

4   Fix a name plate to your front door. The plate should be made out of best quality brass. It should contain your name and your chosen letters. These letters are your 'qualifications' so make sure they stand out.

5   Take off all your clothes.

6   Lie down on the bed.

7   Stick your needle into the back of your ear. Taking off all your clothes means that you won't get any blood on them. You can say 'ouch' if you like.

8   Now stick your needle into the sole of one of your feet. It doesn't matter which. Say 'ouch' again.

9   Now stick your needle into the sole of your other foot. You may say 'ooh' if you are tired of saying 'ouch'.

10 Feel much better.

Dyslexia: how to cope

ETON: *Ljrk finuerh di fgkoplrs ert…yndiof weor!*

Khrkld kdhenn keffn gi leuify bjkks kenyh igth yu kjyds fiey ishg? Ike kjue ityghkk eiuty tnitkh fghyyjk ik ghkii! Kelygh rtyiu gh ookij yut thukkl ogh ikjsm fhyyjk ikolkk fty ih ghkkme – ejdkk tiuhtt. W thjjyt fghew bnui ihhg kliggh mnes (okkhjs jghte – ngghe idsn ih ih) kehfiug, jhkkes ig. Qwtyj idhsj dhuio hj pthei isdio bczu. Ulethhg ngihew hg idhfl idhsj ljgk hfdu hrhjk igfjd jg gh. OGHEJ! Hgjke ihg ehos ohgjd. Iggh ejus hjtjle siff eh wi; tkejj foio. Ighe zdjk widus hjlsiu rhjkw oisu. Ihje osiodk. Huide kjej kkhiif ei bdhejje odke jejs duhs. Chdus tioj eu ehuis kkjes lkis hui.

Hgehe idus iggh syuio eh ighe sidhi fujhke diios.

Fudiow kehjo dhu dhu jeio! Odji eii ikkdj gi leuiffy ieur thkko ifj fty isoijjk.

Everything you need to know about obsessions

It's certainly true that a lot of people are obsessional. They just go on and on about things. They won't let problems go. They have to keep worrying about them.

If, for example, you take a bath just once a day, then you're behaving fairly normally. If, however, you take a bath every hour then some doctors would say that you were exhibiting signs of obsessional behaviour. They'd claim that one bath a day is enough. That might be true, but it is also a fact that germs can be a problem. And some people do agree that a bath every 24 hours might not be enough. Twenty minutes after one bath the germs will be queuing up to get back into position. There are lots of diseases caused by germs. Things like lassa fever, tuber-culosis, pneumonia, influenza, parotitis, malaria, sleeping sickness – all sorts of horrid things. Things that really make you ill. And kill you.

So it might not be silly, after all, to have a bath every few hours. Or even to have one every hour on the hour. Bathing every hour would do more to keep the germs down. And bathing every half hour would give you an even better chance of remaining germ-free. It's always better to be safe than sorry, after all.

It's important to make sure that the gas is always turned off too. If gas taps are switched on and someone comes in with a match in his hand there could be nasty accident. It's easy to make a mistake. It's much safer to check. Between baths.

How to deal with depression, anxiety and nervous disorders

These are minor problems and relatively rare, so we won't spend a great deal of time on them. People who suffer from depression and related illnesses are almost invariably self-centred types whose principal aim is selfishly to draw attention to themselves. Nonetheless, there are some simple remedies to these conditions, so we list them below.

1 Count your blessings.

2 Pull yourself together.

3 Remember that every cloud has a silver lining.

4 Stop feeling sorry for yourself.

5 Keep your chin up.

6 Think of someone less fortunate than yourself.

7 Put a brave face on it.

8 Don't let things get you down.

9 Remember that time is a great healer.

10 Get a grip on yourself.

When and how to make a nice cup of tea

True first aiders know that there is nothing more useful in an emergency than a really nice cup of tea. Making a cup of tea is the first thing that should be done when there is any sort of medical crisis. Road accidents, unexpected childbirth, heart attacks, strokes – all are best treated with a nice cup of tea. If the patient is unconscious then the head should be tilted back and as much tea as possible poured down the throat. Don't worry if some is spilt.

To make a nice cup of tea follow these instructions:

1   Find a large pot, a cup, a saucer, a spoon, a quarter pound packet of tea (not tea bags), a pint of milk, a bowl of sugar, another spoon (smaller than the first spoon). You will also need a kettle and some water.

2   Put the water into the kettle and heat it so that the water boils.

3   Put two large teaspoonfuls of tea into the tea pot (one for the patient and one for the pot – if there are two patients make it three large teaspoonfuls).

4   When the kettle has sung for two minutes pour the boiling water into the tea pot. (Remember, pot to kettle – never kettle to pot.)

5   Put the lid on the tea pot and leave it for 4½ minutes.

6   Pour milk into the cup. The cup should be approximately one fifth full of milk.

7   Pour tea from the tea pot into the cup so that it mixes with the milk.

8   Use a spoon to stir and remove some of the floating tea leaves.

9   Put three teaspoonfuls of sugar into the cup full of tea. Stir again.

10 The tea is now ready to drink. It will be a nice cup of tea.

Bipedal Therapeutics (professional)

Second Aid course

Choosing a source of medical advice

Between 1978 and 1982 the Belgian State Medical Research Organisation funded a programme designed to find out where people obtained their medical advice – and how good that advice turned out to be. Their report ran to 584 pages but can be summarised as follows:

The 45,302 Belgian citizens investigated obtained their medical advice from the following sources:

A doctor	24%
A nurse	18%
A pharmacist	5%
A female relative	11%
A woman round the corner	38%
A magazine	17%
A doctor on a radio phone-in programme	3%
A hairdresser	2%
A piano tuner	0.00001%
A television programme	4%

(The total comes to rather more than 100%. The Belgian

scientists involved in the research programme concluded that this was either because of an arithmetical error or because some of the respondents had lied.)

The quality and accuracy of the advice proffered and accepted was tested by computer and found to be as follows:

Advice from doctor	33% accurate
Advice from nurse	34% accurate
Advice from pharmacist	26% accurate
Advice from female relative	69% accurate
Advice from woman round the corner	93% accurate
Advice from magazine	11% accurate
Advice from doctor on the radio	2% accurate
Advice from hairdresser	17% accurate
Advice from piano tuner	54% accurate
Advice from television programme	0.09% accurate

Finding the right woman round the corner

It is clear from the Belgian research work quoted above, that the best medical advice comes from 'a woman round the corner'. It is, however, important to make sure you've found the correct person. Here is some advice on what to look for.

1   She will wear elastic stockings designed to disguise her varicose veins and prevent her ankles swelling to elephantine proportions. These stockings will be elderly, loose and wrinkled.

2   She will wear a full pinafore (which ties around the neck and the waist). The pinafore will be made of a cotton material – usually but not invariably decorated with a floral print. It will NOT be plastic and it will NOT contain a humorous or rude message.

3   Her hair will contain no fewer than three, and no more than seven, curlers. Fewer than three curlers suggests that she is too careless about her appearance to be a skilled diagnostician. More than seven curlers suggests that she is too interested in herself. She may wear a small, cotton

print headscarf around her hair. If she does then it will be tied in a large knot at the front of her head.

4   Unless pointing at something, she will stand with her arms crossed and resting on her bosom. Her bosom will always be immense.

5   She will have a smouldering, half-smoked, untipped cigarette hanging from her lower lip. She will never be seen to light a cigarette and she will never be seen with a new cigarette in her mouth.

6   When available for consultation she will stand on her front doorstep.

The woman round the corner will never ask a monetary fee for her services. She will, however, expect you to pass on to her any secrets, gossip or intimate information you might have. She will expect a full and accurate account of your economic status, your husband's sexual tastes, your family prospects, your plans for the purchase of soft furnishings and any impending court appearances.

Going to the doctor

This is a complicated procedure containing many pitfalls. You must decide a week in advance exactly when you want to fall ill. Ring and make a suitable appointment. Your doctor will be away on holiday. You should be pleased about this because it means that he will be relaxed when you see him next.

When you go to the surgery take with you a packet of sandwiches, a flask, a blow up cushion and the collected works of some prolific novelist.

When you finally get in to see the doctor give him your name as soon as you sit down. He will pretend to know this anyway but he will be lying. If you do not give him your name there is a real risk that he will treat you for someone else's disease. This can be hazardous to your health.

After your visit to the doctor you will want to complain. This is best done in local shops. Stand by the fresh vegetable counter of any small store and say quietly 'My doctor doesn't understand me.' People will immediately stop and talk to you. This will enable you to damage your doctor's reputation far more effectively than if you complain through official channels.

Medical examinations: the two main types

Different types of patient obviously require different types of medical examination. Patients can, by and large, be expected to be divided into two groups.

1 Group One

Includes men of all ages, women under the age of 16 and women over the age of 25. The normal examination required takes thirty-five seconds and consists of a cursory tap at the chest and a quick peep down the throat.

2 Group Two

Includes women aged between 16 and 25. Because of the peculiar disorders which can sometimes affect patients in this sex and age category, a full 45 minutes physical examination is always required. (Unless a woman doctor is visited. Women doctors are so incompetent that they do not understand the necessity for this type of examination.) The examination performed on Group Two patients will be designed to provide the examining physician with as much information as possible about the health and status of the patient's reproductive organs and breasts. It will always be necessary for the patient to remove all her clothes. It may be necessary for the doctor to remove his clothes too.

Types of doctor available

Type A: middle-aged, balding, rumpled, overweight, male

If you cannot find the woman round the corner then he is your next best bet. You can recognise Type A doctors in many ways. He will shamble, look extremely untidy and have a droopy nicotine stained moustache. He will drive an elderly battered motor car which he will park in such a way that other drivers will be uncertain whether to pass on the left or the right. His equipment will consist of a leaky fountain pen and a stethoscope which has at least a yard of red rubber tubing connecting two old fashioned ear pieces to a funny little piece of cold, rusty metal. The tubing will usually have been patched with a bicycle repair outfit. He will wear a tweed jacket and indescribable trousers. His brown brogues will need cleaning. During the summer months he will wear a tweed overcoat and a tweed fishing hat which he will always leave behind when he has visited a patient at home. The Type A doctor is technically incompetent but completely out of date and therefore relatively safe. His rough, blustery manner will hide a heart of gold and a mind of lead. Years of experience will enable him to offer useful bits and pieces of advice. He will unlikely to send a patient to hospital unless the alternative is bound to be a visit from the undertaker.

Type B: young. well dressed, eager, thin, male

To be honest you'd probably be better off waiting for a call to be put through to the phone-in doctor on the local radio. Or you might try writing to one of the magazines that have a resident nurse. The Type B doctor will drive a small foreign car that has a green flashing light attached to the roof. He may wear a white coat when dispensing advice in the consulting room. He will wear a two or three piece suit and carry a huge array of pens in his inside jacket pocket. He will carry several large, black, plastic briefcases crammed with bits and pieces of medical equipment. Many of these will have plugs at one end and will require electricity. The Type B doctor is, to put it bluntly, a lethal menace. He will read all the medical journals, be able to spell several modern drugs and be taking part in at least two sponsored drug trials (that's where all the equipment comes from). He'll send you to hospital at the drop of a beat and refer you for a stack of blood tests if you as much as sneeze. Best avoided.

Type C: female

Independent scientific research has shown that female doctors are always humourless, earnest and extremely plain. They never smile. If they had been born better looking they would, of course, have grown up to become nurses and then they would have had something to smile about. They wear expensive clothes (usually navy blue suits with white blouses) extremely badly and are always unnervingly punctual. They can be quite good when dealing with pre-menstrual tension and some menopausal problems but in general their skills are more theoretical than practical. Like Type B doctors they always carry cases full of medical equipment around with them. They can often pronounce quite difficult medical words without much of a stutter but their diagnostic skills are usually negligible. Their brains are usually as big as their breasts which are not usually very big at all. A visit to the hairdressers will usually provide better medical advice than a visit to the Type C doctor.

The answers to the questions no one ever dares ask the doctor

No
No
Yes
Maybe
Perhaps
No
Yes
Yes
Yes
Never
Sometimes
Only after meals
No

No
No
Certainly not
I don't know
Yes
Yes
No

The 101 questions female patients most commonly ask male doctors

Is there anything you can do about this? What is it? Is it infectious? Will I have to take time off work? Can I have a sick note please? Is there any charge for that? Can I have another sick note for my insurance company? Would you please look at this while I'm here? Is it going to get worse? Is it anything to worry about? Does it always do that? Is it dangerous? Need I worry? Should I tell my mother? Do you have to? Will it help? Do I have to take everything off?

Is it always this cold in here? Did you mean absolutely everything? What are you going to do with that? Is it a necessary part of the examination? Is this what you meant? Would you please stop that? Would you please do that again?

Would you move a little that way? Would you move a little this way? Are you a proper doctor? Did you? Have you ever done that before? Do you do this every time? Where did you get that scar? Did it hurt? Would you turn the light on please? Would you look away for a moment? Would you please stop that? Would you turn the light off again, please? Would you wait until the light is off? Why won't you put the light off? Now what are you doing? Where on earth did you learn that? Is it dangerous? Will it hurt? Are you sure it won't hurt? Is it safe? Will you do it again please? Would you please stop for a moment?

Would you do it again now? Would you unfasten that zip?

Would you please move that? Would you take it out now? Would you rub just here? Would you rub just there, too? Would you hand me a tissue please? Would you hand me another tissue? Would you pass that waste bin? Would you stop that? Would you wait a moment? Would you please stop? Now will you do it? What are you trying? What did you say? What is that? When? How? Where? For how long? How long? Isn't that a record? Should I rub it or leave it alone? Can I help? Would you like me to do this? Or that? Or shall I pull this? Have you ever seen anything like it? Do you like it? Do I have to give up sex? Do you mean that? Do you want to? Will you be gentle? Why is it always so difficult to get an appointment? What do you think now? What was that noise? Was it the receptionist? Was it the nurse? Should I put my clothes on? Should you put your clothes on? Where are they? Is this yours? Whose are these? What is this? Who is she? When was that? Would you please fasten that? Would you hold this? Would you stop doing that? Would you hurry?

How often do I have to take them? Can I take them with alcohol? When should I come and see you again? Would you like me to wear the red ones?

Decoding phrases used by doctors

Doctors are always reluctant to use diagnostic labels which sound too commonplace. It is difficult to justify an expensive training and a large fee if the patient realises that his mother was right after all.

This short directory is designed to tell you nothing useful. Everything here is inaccurate and useless. If you want to learn what big words mean, go and spend six years at medical school.

erythropoietic photoporphyria = queasy
interstitial pulmonary fibrosis = warts
hypogammaglobulinaemia = bunions
membranous glomerulonephritis = under the weather

anaphylactoid purpura = a chill on the kidneys
kyphoscoliosis = dicky ticker
superficial venous thrombosis = funny turn
hepatomegaly = worms
subacute bacterial endocarditis = proper poorly
polycythaemia rubra vera = gastric stomach

Decoding hospital idiom

If you've ever phoned a hospital to enquire about the health of a loved one, you'll have probably been puzzled by the reply. What does 'satisfactory' mean? And how comfortable is 'comfortable'?

Well, here are the official medical explanations for those words and phrases that hospital spokesmen and spokeswomen use with such relish.

'Had a good day' = he spent 90 minutes in the bathroom and Nurse Barton came out with her uniform buttoned up the wrong way.

'Comfortable' = lots of really good bowel movements today.

'Satisfactory' = he's opened his bowels once today.

'Improving' = he's opened his bowels more often than yesterday.

'Stable' = we're not quite sure where he is at the moment but he's bound to be around here somewhere.

'Poorly' = he hasn't opened his bowels for two days.

'Critical' = no bowel movements for a week. May actually be dead but the doctor hasn't been round today so we can't be sure.

How to find a good optician

Go straight along the High Street and turn left just after the Post Office. Take the first right after the laundry and go straight past the little alley which leads down to that old warehouse that was converted into a night club two years ago. There was a murder there last year. Two blokes got into a fight over a woman. Anyway, go past the alley and keep on going past the road that comes after it. I can't remember the name but there are some traffic lights there, and there's a baker's on the corner. It's either a baker's or a shoe-shop. Turn left at the Chinese take-away – it's actually on the other side of the road. At least it used to be a Chinese take-away. I think they moved. It's a video shop now, I think. Turn left there and go right down that road as far as you can. When you get to the end you'll see the canal in front of you. No, I tell a lie, it's the railway cutting. Go left there and walk along the bank. Then look for a left hand turning that has a pub on one corner and a sweet shop on the other. It's about the third turning on the left. Third or fourth. Go about a hundred yards along and look for a tiny little road that needs repairing. There's a cobbler's about two doors down. Go about a hundred and fifty yards up that road and there are three shops in a cul-de-sac. I think one of those is a good optician.

How to choose a nursing home for a relative

1   The first decision to be made concerns the cost of the home. Naturally, if you are paying for the accommodation yourself you will want to find the cheapest place available. This is also true, of course, if the cost of the home is likely to come from monies which might otherwise have been left to you in a will. You must, however, be careful not to choose a home which is so unpleasant that your legacy might be threatened.

2   Always choose a nursing home which is at least six miles away from the nearest railway station, bus stop or taxi rank. If transport is too readily available then your relative will

find it easy to escape from the home. This can involve you in extra expense and cause considerable embarrassment.

3 Make sure that the facilities for making external telephone calls are not readily available. Ignore this rule and you'll be getting calls twice a day. Your relative will also be able to telephone for a taxi and make an escape that way.

4 Always try and choose a nursing home that has large, rambling grounds. To begin with your relative will find this an attractive feature. Talk about the advantages of spacious acres and point out how pleasant it will be in the summer. Only when he or she has been there for a few weeks will your relative realise that it is impossible to enlist the help of passers-by when planning an escape.

5 Choose a nursing home that is approached by a long, narrow country road. If the road goes over a hill or two then that is better still. For six months of the year the roads are likely to be impassable and you won't be able to visit the home.

6 Try to find a nursing home staffed entirely by foreigners. Your relative will find it difficult to send messages to the outside world.

7 Make sure that the nursing home serves large portions of good food. Fat, stodgy relatives are far less likely to make a break for it than thin, hungry ones. It is also a fact that thin relatives live much longer than fat ones, and the cost of providing accommodation for those extra years will far outweigh the cost of additional food.

Introductory Guide to Disasters and Emergencies

Dealing with life threatening predicaments

A flood

1 Make sure that all your financial records and details of outstanding debts are lost in the flood. Your home insurance policy, on the other hand, should be wrapped in a plastic bag and strapped to the outside of your chimney pot.

2 Drag all your good furniture upstairs and all your old furniture downstairs. Do the same with your carpets.

3 Keep an elderly female relative, a baby or a pregnant woman in an upstairs bedroom. If things get really bad and the flood water rises beyond a joke, you'll be able to ensure speedy attention from the emergency services.

4 Be certain to keep a full daily journal. After the flood has receded you'll want to sell your story. A daily diary will provide you with something to offer to the Reader's Digest. If you have a camera handy then take some pictures as the water pours in through the front door. These can be sold via an agency to newspapers around the world.

5 Rip your bath free of its fixtures and fittings, glue the plug into position and set off down your street to visit old ladies.

Use a breadboard or an umbrella as a paddle. This will get you a good spot on the television news and ensure that your story will later fetch a high price. Try to rescue someone if you can – preferably a crippled pensioner or a half-naked girl with enormous breasts.

Locusts

You must destroy the eggs laid by the invading swarms of locusts. There are several ways in which you can do this but the traditional approach – knocking the top off each egg with a teaspoon – is probably still the best.

Nuclear attack

1 First you must remember that the purpose of the four minute warning is to give you plenty of time to prepare yourself properly for the nuclear attack. The government has spent many millions of pounds on buying special 'early warning equipment' so that you will be able to make your own arrangements with time to spare. So don't waste those precious minutes. Use them to the full!

2 Sand bags are a very effective way to build a protective barrier. And they'll also help to keep out the looters after the attack has finished. You can easily make your own. All you need are a few simple household supplies. Plastic carrier bags will make suitable containers, for example. So will dustbin liners. You'll also need two or three tons of sand. Builder's sand will do perfectly well, though some might prefer a finer grain. 'Sharp' sand is a superior type and easy to obtain.

3 Sand is effective against blast and looters, but to protect yourself against nuclear radiation you really need to line your home with lead. You probably don't have many sheets of lead to hand but please don't despair. You can

build yourself a very effective lead shield by using ordinary lead pencils. You'll need about twenty-two million ordinary pencils to shield the average living room. 4H pencils are best because they are the hardest. Blunt the ends of all the pencils and then weave them into a sort of wattle fence. You can use glue if you like but do remember that you've only got four minutes so you can't rely on products that need five minutes to set.

4   Put up a notice outside your house announcing that you have declared yourself a Nuclear Free Zone. This may not work if the people who are aiming the missiles can't see your notice but at least you'll be able to bring a civil action in the International Court after the hostilities have finished: it is almost certain that your notice will provide you with a sound basis for a 'restoration of domicility' suit.

5   Put spots of glue all over your body and stick leaves onto the glue. Then dig a shallow trench in your garden. If your defences prove inadequate and your sand bags fail to keep out the blast then run outside and lie down in your trench. This will ensure that your little part of the world will be left neat and tidy after the war has finished.

An aeroplane crash (pilot's guide)

1   Use the intercom system to tell the passengers that everything is going to be fine, that you've got a slight, technical problem but that things will be OK. Tell a joke if you can remember one. The passengers will appreciate your interest and good humour and those that survive will probably buy you dinner once a year for the rest of their lives. You only have to be involved in 365 crashes to eat free forever.

2   Tell the prettiest stewardess to come forward into the cabin or control room or whatever you call it. If you're going to crash in some remote place you'll need company, and you

may as well have first choice of the best crumpet on board.

3   Loosen your tie and rumple your hair. Nothing annoys passengers more than climbing out of a wrecked aeroplane only to see the captain jump out looking fresh and smart.

4   Say all sorts of useful and impressive things to your co-pilot: 'The auto-lift propeller on the starboard engine has collapsed', or 'There's been an electrical failure in the forward galley', or 'We've got a fractured tail fin gyro compass'. This will all be recorded and therefore be available to any subsequent investigators. You will have established beyond any reasonable doubt that the aeroplane was the cause of the crash and not bad driving.

An aeroplane crash (passenger's guide)

1   Hold tight to your hand luggage. There are bound to be some dishonest passengers on board who will steal your camera or overnight bag.

2   Ask for a refund if you've bought any duty free drink or perfume. The chances are that the bottle will break if your aeroplane crashes and you'll have a devil of a game getting the airline to recompense you for the loss.

3   Sit next to the emergency exit. If there is someone already sitting there ask him or her to move. Make sure that you're within reach of the door handle by the time the plane crashes.

4   Put little bits of cotton wool into your ears. People will be screaming a great deal. In addition, the noise at the moment of impact can be tremendous.

5   Remove any fountain pens from your pocket. The change in air pressure can result in ink leaking onto your clothes. Airline companies are often reluctant to pay dry cleaning

bills after a major crash. Wrap the pens in individual plastic bags and give them to the stewardess to hold. Make sure that she gives you a full receipt, signed and dated.

Acne

1   If you have a lot of nasty looking spots then you can try covering them up with pieces of sticking plaster. Claim that you have been in a road accident and that your face has been badly cut. If you only have one or two spots in the 'beard' region, then you can cover them with bits of toilet tissue. Stain the toilet tissue red and claim that you cut yourself shaving. (This excuse is more suitable for men than for women.)

2   The other real alternative is to keep a low profile. Stay in the house until the spots have gone. This may mean becoming a hermit for nine or ten years but even that is better than having to go out in public with spots on your face. Nothing looks worse.

Plague

1   Make yourself a gruesome mask and wear it all the time. This won't actually stop you getting the plague, of course, but it will scare the shit out of everyone who sees you. People in the Middle Ages used to wear masks like this because it kept everyone else at a safe distance.

2   Buy hundreds of tins of baked beans and ravioli and soup. This will save you having to visit shops and mixing with the hordes of sick people littering the pavements.

3   Keep a big bonfire burning in your garden. Any clothing (or relatives) likely to be contaminated should be thrown onto this bonfire as soon as they become suspect.

Being marooned on a desert island

If you think you're likely to be stuck on a desert island you must know what to take with you. Here is a list of eight suggestions:

1   An inflatable boat with outboard motor and 10,000 gallons of fuel. You probably won't want to escape from your island but a small boat will make a handy runabout. If you think you're likely to be trapped on a fairly flat island, free of vegetation, then you might like to take a small hovercraft instead.

2   One gross of Christmas hampers from Fortnum and Mason. Those big hampers have all sorts of goodies in them and buying supplies this way will save a lot of shopping. Have the hampers delivered straight to the island.

3   A million cans of assorted beers and lagers. Don't take only one brand; you might grow tired of it.

4   A refrigerator to keep the beer in.

5   A rough-rider motor bike for moving about on the island. Together with lots of two-stroke fuel.

6   A Swiss army penknife for chopping down trees and making a house.

7   Another million cans of assorted beers and lagers.

8   A record player for renting out to the stupid idiots who are already on the island and have nothing with them but eight gramophone records.

Social Studies

Exploring and understanding human
relationships and behavioural patterns

How to be a welcome car passenger

Driving a car is easy. Any fool can do it. It is far more difficult to be a useful and effective passenger. And yet people are allowed to travel as passengers without any training at all!

Listed below are some tips and hints for would-be passengers who want to make themselves really welcome.

1   Always fasten your seat belt the instant you get into a car. Make sure that it is tightly buckled and check the anchorage points.

2   Help the driver by looking out for approaching traffic. Tell him if you see anything coming up behind, or if you see any pedestrians in the distance.

3   Remind him to check his fuel gauge. And remind him about oil, water and air for the tyres too. All drivers appreciate this sort of help.

4   Adjust the driving mirror for him. If you can't see out of it properly then the chances are that he can't either.

5   If you think he ought to be braking more often, try to offer subtle hints – such as pressing really hard with your foot on

the floor. Straighten your leg so that he can see what you are doing. It is rather bad form to say anything directly to him, but it's perfectly acceptable to drop a clever hint like this.

6   Offer useful and constructive advice about motoring in general and about his car in particular. Say things like:

"Does that noise worry you a lot?"

"You could probably get another 20mph out of this by fitting a Quorg Carburettor."

"Have you thought about buying an automatic?"

"They don't make cars like this any more do they?"

Read a few motoring magazines and you'll soon be able to make up new comments and questions of your own. Remember that car drivers love to talk about their own cars!

7   If you know the road ahead then do share your expert knowledge with the driver. Tell him when to expect traffic lights, pedestrian crossings and radar speed traps. He'll appreciate your help.

Breast shape: a key to personality

Research in Sweden has shown that it is possible to judge the personality of a woman by examining the shape of her breasts. Teams of psychologists in Gotenburg have recently published a series of scientific papers in which they have provided conclusive evidence in support of their theory.

Here are some of their conclusions:

Small and pert

The owner is likely to be lively, alert and intelligent. Probably rather extrovert and certainly ambitious. She will enjoy sports and favour an independent existence.

Small but droopy

This individual will be shy, easily upset and sensitive. She will find sexual relationships difficult and she will probably seek a career where she can share her sense of compassion with others. She will have an artistic nature and will enjoy literature and music.

Large and firm

Women with breasts of this type are confident and sure of themselves. They enjoy leading others, like to feel that they are at the centre of things, and will initiate new friendships quite regularly. They enjoy being admired and take particular pleasure in the attentions of members of the opposite sex.

Very large and quite firm

The woman with breasts of this type will be imaginative, thoughtful and appreciative. She will enjoy good food, be keen to take great care of her family and will obtain great pleasure from sports of all kinds. She will be vivacious, understanding and sexually aggressive. She will also be demanding and will not easily take 'no' for an answer.

Very large and droopy

These breasts usually belong to a woman who is kind, loving and generous. She will share her love with all those around her and will enjoy a great number of open and stimulating relationships.

Computer dating guide

Lonely? Searching for a friend? Looking for a lover? Desperate for sex? Before you approach a computer dating agency or start to hunt through the lonely hearts columns you must find out just what those personal advertisements really mean...

Compassionate = Easy lay

Homely = Desperate to get married, acquire two children and a kitchen full of pans. In order to achieve this aim is willing to allow fully clothed body to be fondled.

Vivacious = Spotty with lank, greasy hair.

Slim = Anorexic.

Cuddly = Grossly obese. Breasts, thighs and abdomen will be disgustingly disfigured with hideous stretch marks. There will be ugly red rashes hiding in unexpected places.

Good looking = A good looking man will be effeminate and petite. A good looking woman will have strong angular features.

Athletic = Athletic men have muscles on their muscles and talk incessantly about their modest sporting successes. They wear boxer shorts and like jogging in the rain. Athletic women are even worse. They have verrucae on their ears.

Sensual = Expensive.

Uncomplicated = Stupid.

Warm = Possessive.

Divorced = Randy as hell.

Shy = Catatonic.

Sensitive = Always bursting into tears.

Mature = Geriatric. Frail and probably slightly disabled. Often incontinent.

Friendly = has herpes.

Attentive = Jealous.

Decisive = Overbearing.

Handsome = Handsome men are raging poofters. Handsome women are dykes.

Independent = Selfish.

Intelligent = Boring.

Sophisticated = Snobbish.

Middle Class = Poor.

Upper Class = Very poor.

Rugged = Ugly.

Looking for permanent relationship = Homeless.

Generous = Demanding.

Witty = Likely to be embarrassing in public.

Pretty = Simple-minded. Spends hours doing her hair and putting on her make-up. Invariably late for dates.

Ambitious = Willing to trade sexual favours in return for professional advancement.

Curvaceous = Fat. Unsuitable for sports cars.

Pleasant = Plain and boring.

Small gifts for the weekend guest to leave behind

1 A simple introductory cookery book full of basic recipes for 'down to earth' and unambitious cooking.

2 A non-stick frying pan.

3 A presentation set of assorted light bulbs – two 60 watt, two 100 watt and two 150 watt.

4 A tin of 'extra strong' bath cleanser for 'removing those ugly brown stains'.

5 A boar's hair lavatory brush.

6 One jar of instant coffee and a small tin of powdered milk.

7 A do-it-yourself plumbing kit.

8 A small tin of hinge oil.

9 A combined cork screw and bottle opener.

10 Several yards of plastic draught excluder.

Small gifts for the morning after

If you've spent the night with someone and you want to leave them a small 'thank you' gift, then choose something from this list of suggestions:

1 A small book on how to choose names for babies.

2   A comprehensive textbook on baby care.

3   A small, illustrated book on venereology.

4   A book on sexual technique, complete with introductory drawings.

5   A complete set of polaroid prints bound in a small plastic folder.

6   A tooth care kit – including toothbrush, toothpaste and antiseptic mouthwash.

7   An under arm deodorant spray with matching toilet soap.

8   A hot water bottle.

9   A book on wedding etiquette.

10 A large sociological study of the causes and consequences of deviant behaviour.

What every woman should carry in her handbag

Face powder, vanity mirror, fountain pen, propelling pencil, diary, address book, lipstick, spare lipstick, eyebrow tweezers, house key, car keys, key to parents' home, sunglasses, spare sunglasses, refill for fountain pen, another spare lipstick, nail polish (two colours), nail varnish remover, local telephone directory, box of matches, cigarette lighter, eye make-up, safety pin, ball point pen, comb, manicure set in small plastic wallet, tortoiseshell hair brush, typewriter ribbon, opera glasses, kitchen scissors, one small gold ear-ring, silver bracelet, last year's diary, sewing kit, spare pair of tights, unused but slightly grubby loose tampon, tampon applicator, street map of Brussels, scrap of paper with recipe for cheese flavoured shortbread, Italian phrase book, packet of paper tissues, spare pair of knickers, two yards of loose elastic, photographs of family, photograph of self in bikini at age 16, textbook on elementary nuclear physics, book of matches from the Athens Hilton, packet of mints, rain hood, packet of cough sweets, folding umbrella, packet of instant cake mix, antacid tablets, half used packet of birth control pills, bottle of patent slimming pills, battery powered vibrator, spare button from sleeve of man's sports jacket, loose zip, calorie counting booklet, small box containing rock hard piece of wedding cake, small silver horseshoe from piece of wedding cake, two spare batteries for vibrator, another spare lipstick.

What every man should carry in his pockets

House key, car keys, handkerchief, money, penknife, packet of condoms.

Urban Anthropology

A basic guide to children, parents, marriage and families

Bringing up children

Children need firm handling and plenty of the right sort of foodstuffs. The secret of firm handling is to be sure that your child knows who the boss is! Any child who is disobedient should be locked in a broom cupboard for two hours and then sent to bed without any supper.

When your child is good, make sure he has plenty of the foodstuffs he needs. He should have cabbage, spinach, cauliflower, mashed potatoes, lumpy gravy, tapioca and rice pudding every day.

Why pets are better than children

If you've been wondering whether to add a child or a pet to your family then this section will help you make a decision.

1   You can put pets into kennels when you want to go on holiday. Children usually have to be taken with you. This entails extra expense and can change the whole nature of holidaymaking.

2   Children need to be educated. This is a tiresome and often expensive process. You may need to help with homework.

This will probably include geometry, Latin and adverbs.

3   Children need clothes and shoes. Animals do not.

4   Pets don't have to be taken to parties. And they never ring you up in the middle of the night weeping inconsolably.

5   Pets don't squabble about which TV programme to watch.

6   Pets (particularly goldfish) don't have to be washed, taken to the dentist or taught how to behave at table.

7   Children will want pocket money but pets never ask for anything.

Are you related to your parents?

Many people suspect that they might have been adopted by their so-called parents. The following short quiz is designed to help you discover the truth about your parentage.

1   Do you have the same colour hair as:

a) your father

b) your mother

c) both parents

2   Do you have the same colour eyes as:

a) your father

b) your mother

c) both parents

3   Do you have the same colour skin as:

a) your father

b) your mother

c) both parents

4   Do you enjoy the same hobbies as:

a) your father

b) your mother

c) both parents

5   Are you approximately the same height as:

   a) your father

   b) your mother

   c) both parents

6   Do you have the same general body shape as:

   a) your father

   b) your mother

   c) both parents

7   Do you take the same shoe size as:

   a) your father

   b) your mother

   c) both parents

8   Do you like the same films as:

   a) your father

   b) your mother

   c) both parents

9   Do you have the same sort of job as:

   a) your father

   b) your mother

   c) both parents

CONCLUSION

If you answered YES to all the a) questions, you are related to your father.

If you answered YES to all the b) questions, you are related to your mother.

If you answered YES to all the c) questions, you are related to both parents.

If you answered NO to some or all of the a) questions, you are not related to the person you call 'father'.

If you answered NO to some or all of the b) questions, you are not related to the person you call 'mother'.

If you answered NO to some or all of the c) questions, you are not related to either of the people you think of as parents.

Domestic violence:
suggested rules and regulations

NOTE: *The following advice is not suitable for anyone and should be ignored (like the rest of this damned book).*

Surveys done by teams of eminent female doctors have shown that every wife in the world runs a 15.6% risk of being murdered by her husband. Surveys done by equally reputable male doctors have shown that every husband runs a 34.5% risk of being murdered by his wife. Cumulative figures show that the total number of wives murdered in 1982 came to just under 4 million while the total number of husbands murdered reached a staggering 8.5 million.

In an attempt to reduce the number of deaths resulting from ordinary domestic violence the International Marriage Guidance Association has produced a list of basic guidelines.

1   When two partners in a relationship are in a close grappling situation and one partner weighs over fourteen pounds more than the other, then the heavier partner shall be restricted to the use of one hand or arm at a time.

2   Feet shall not be used in combat unless they are naked and the toe nails have been trimmed within the previous 7 days. Any partner attacking the other with feet encased in heavy shoes or shoes with high heels shall be reported to the Disciplinary Committee of the International Marriage Guidance Association.

3   Any female partner who has finger nails that extend beyond her finger for more than 3mm shall be required to wear leather, woollen or sheepskin gloves throughout the period of violence.

4   If weapons are to be used in close-combat situations, then the partners shall restrict themselves as follows: neither partner shall pick up any object weighing more than 1.75 kilos and nor shall either partner pick up and use any

weapon which is more than 27cm in length.

5 If objects are being used as missiles then neither partner shall throw anything weighing more than half as much as the other partner's head. Missiles shall not be thrown at more than 30 miles per hour and professional ball players shall not throw missiles at all. If either partner recognises would-be missiles of great monetary value then the cry 'HOLD' shall be uttered clearly and without delay; the partner about to use that missile shall give up the object and allow it to be put in a safe place. The partner deprived of his or her missile shall, however, be then allowed, without let or hindrance, to choose, pick up and take aim with, another object of similar weight and proportions.

6 Neither partner shall bleed on damask covers, valuable first editions, polar bear rugs, silk dressing gowns or fitted carpets. If any partner shall accidentally bleed on such surfaces then a delay shall be ordered while the offending stain is dealt with.

7 If either partner picks up a knife, blade, piece of cutlery, razor, penknife, scalpel, lancet, chisel, hatchet, axe, pick, cleaver, cutting instrument of any kind, scissors, shears, scythe, bodkin, needle or pike then the other partner shall be entitled to call 'TIME OUT' until he or she has dressed in armour.

8 Firearms are not allowed in ordinary domestic violence.

Happy divorcing

Statistics show that 89% of all marriages end in divorce. If you are faced with divorce, completely ignore this programme of advice:

1 As soon as the divorce is inevitable a Committee of Division should be formed.

2 The Committee of Division shall consist of five friends of

the husband, five friends of the wife, five relatives of the husband, five relatives of the wife, five public notaries, five former boyfriends of the wife, five former girlfriends of the husband, five current boyfriends of the wife, five current girlfriends of the husband, five completely impartial bystanders who know nothing at all about either partner, five tradesmen who can talk about the husband with affection and respect, five tradesmen who can talk about the wife with affection and respect, five qualified quantity surveyors, five auctioneers, five bankers, five certified public accountants, five jewellery experts, five insurance assessors and five dental surgeons.

3 In payment for their services the members of the Committee of Division shall be entitled to share no less than 75% and no more than 85% of the value of the joint estate.

4 The Committee of Division shall be given complete authority to share the chattels, stocks, provisions, resources, revenues, wherewithals, means, appliances, conveniences, utensils, conveyances, organs, plants, fittings, appointments, furniture, paraphernalia, impedimenta, baggage, effects, goods, appurtenances, equipage, traps, property, assets, belongings, homes, domains, demesnes, farms, plantations, ranches, estates, cottages, houses, flats, apartments, realms, kingdoms and spheres of the two erstwhile partners. They shall decide which partner shall have entitlement to which chattels, stocks, provisions, resources, revenues, wherewithals, means, appliances, conveniences, utensils, conveyances, organs, plants, fittings, appointments, furniture, paraphernalia, impedimenta, baggage, effects, goods, appurtenances, equipage, traps, property, assets, belongings, homes, domains, demesnes, farms, plantations, ranches, estates, cottages, caravans, houses, flats, apartments, realms, kingdoms and spheres.

5 Once the Committee of Division has made its decisions the two partners shall accept the decision without dissent. If

either partner dissents then the other partner shall be entitled to refer the matter to a LAWYER. The partner in dissent shall not be entitled to obtain the services of a LAWYER and shall therefore be stripped clean and thrown to the wolves.

6   The Committee of Division shall also be empowered to make rulings about the allocation of spiritual resources, access to children, the publication of memoirs, the future sexual behaviour of the two partners and the amount of ill-founded and malicious gossip to be allowed.

7. If there be any dispute then the Committee of Division's decision shall be final and wholly binding.

N.B. The Committee of Division shall have no jurisdiction over items of personal aid and support such as contact lenses, spectacles, silicone implants, trusses, hearing aids, walking sticks, vaginal and anal dilators, vibrators (where these have been used as personal rather than community items), steel hip replacements, artificial heart valves, pacemakers, vein transplants, dentures (partial or complete), or any other items of a similarly personal nature. These shall be considered as the exclusive property of the individual concerned.

Quirk, Trait and Foible Analysis

Self analysis

Computerised personality check

Most intelligent readers regard traditional horoscopes with scepticism. Too often the forecasts which are made bear little resemblance to reality and the forecasters themselves owe their successes to luck rather than scientific skill.

This unique computerised personality check has been devised by a team of skilled crypto-scientists and is designed to enable you to check your future prospects with the aid of specially prepared tests.

Some of these check-tests may confuse you but please do not be alarmed or worried by the questions.

Answer each question in turn and add up your score with the aid of your home computer.* Then use the computerised personality check table.

Sign of the Zodiac	Your basic point score
Aquarius	1
Pisces	2
Aries	3
Taurus	4

---

* You may use a pencil and a piece of paper if your home computer is afunctional.

Gemini	5
Cancer	6
Leo	7
Virgo	8
Libra	9
Scorpio	10
Sagittarius	11
Capricorn	12

Which of these do you prefer?	*Points to add*
Embroidery	3
Football	5
Scotch	2
Whistling	1
Walking	4
Underwater swimming	7

Were you breast fed?
If the answer is YES, add 6 points
If the answer is NO, subtract 6 points

Which of these is your favourite food?	*Points to add*
Asparagus	3
Cottage pie	4
Strawberry jam	5
Whelks	8
Turbot	5
Salmon	3
Mushrooms	1
Cabbage	10
Chips	4
Tuna	7
Truffles	2
Peanut butter	4
Jelly beans	10

Can you drive a motor car?
If the answer is YES, add 2 points
If the answer is NO, subtract 2 points

What is your favourite colour?	Points to add
Red	4
Crimson	3
Blue	3
Purple (light)	5
Pink	4
Black	12
Off white	5
Puce	3
Beige	1
Purple (dark)	9
Indigo	5
Cream	9
Brown	3
Yellow	4
Green	6
Khaki	7
White	2
Violet	3

Would you rather be...?	Points to add
a racing driver	6
a stripper	5
a politician	3
a millionaire	7
a hurdler	11
an aunt or uncle	8
a school teacher	4
a prize fighter	13
a social worker	29

N.B. Choose only one of these.

Which of these is your favourite smell?	Points to add
newly-mown grass	4
freshly baked bread	7
hot tar	4

salt water	3
horse sweat	5
boar pheromone	6

N.B. Choose only one of these.

Your score

To find out what the future holds for you read off the appropriate forecast according to your accumulated score.

Score 3-16

Foot hygiene is likely to be a real problem and those closest to you will turn away in your time of need. Personal relationships will be at a low ebb, mainly due to your own attitudes. Your doctor will prescribe tranquillisers but these will prove sadly inadequate. Industrial disputes will ensure that your financial future remains bleak.

Score 18-28

You are likely to contract a painful infectious disease. You should save money now so that you will be able to cope with the long period of unemployment that is ahead. Your dearest friend will betray you and someone you are destined never to meet will cause havoc in your home. Personal possessions will be lost. Bad weather will damage your roof and make gardening a pointless exercise. You will have cause to regret your failure to maintain insurance premiums.

Score 29-40

Remember that it is not true that things can only get better. You will be surprised at just how much worse they can get. Sinus troubles will persist and varicose veins will be troublesome.

Score 41-45

The garden fence will need attention. This will not be a good time to waste money on yourself. The garden gate will also need repairing. The heating will break down at an inconvenient moment. Take great care in financial matters because you will not have time to deal with them in the future. Halitosis will continue to be a real problem.

Score 46-67

This is not a good time to enter into any business relationship. Relatives will cause emotional turmoil and someone you cherish will suffer irreversible heart damage. Do not allow yourself to be left alone for you may do something 'silly' while depressed. Keep an eye on your friends. Your pets will need surgery. Do your best to stay smart at all times.

Score 68-74

A hospital stay may prove longer than anticipated and financial matters will provide many headaches. It may be wise to take a long holiday abroad. Make urgent repairs to all of your guttering and keep vaccinations up to date. Varicose veins and birthmarks will figure prominently. Beware of men carrying violin cases.

Score 75-89

You will be changing your immediate environment in the near future. Others will look after cooking and heating arrangements, but toilet facilities will be primitive and opportunities for social drinking will be slight. You will have few chances to meet members of the opposite sex, though there will be plenty of time to regret an impromptu physical intimacy.

Score 90-8100

Although apparently generous, redundancy money will soon prove inadequate. Do not plan far ahead. Make sure that your insurance policies are kept up to date. Your toe nails will need trimming and bunions may need special care. Plan travel arrangements to a country where coffee is a major export. Investments made in good faith will prove unwise. Catarrh will continue to be a problem.

What do dreams mean?

There are only six basic dream patterns and these are listed below together with interpretative notes. If your dream does not fit into one of these categories then the only explanation is that your personality has become so disturbed that your theta brain wave pattern has been overwhelmed. This is a serious and irreversible condition.

Dream pattern 1

You are at a cocktail party. Everyone else is dressed in formal evening attire but you are quite naked. You are struggling to cope with a glass of white wine and a plateful of canapes without spilling either food or wine on the host's priceless Persian carpet. Towards the end of the dream you panic as you realise that your toe nails have not been trimmed for over a week. The other guests are staring at them.

The explanation is that you are cruelly repressed. It is likely that your problems started in childhood. Your parents were probably overbearing and demanding and may have pushed you too hard when you were at school. You badly need to express yourself sexually.

Dream pattern 2

You are locked in a telephone kiosk which is being battered by millions of angry butterflies. The telephone does not work and so you cannot call for help.

The explanation is that your financial problems are depressing you. Your inability to satisfy your materialistic ambitions has added to your innate lack of self-discipline. You feel unable to control your savage, animal instincts and fear the eventual consequences.

Dream pattern 3

You are lost in a huge supermarket which is situated inside a vast, covered shopping precinct. You have left your car in a nearby multi-storey car park. Every time you try to leave the supermarket you find yourself in a narrow alleyway full of dustbins. If you do eventually succeed in getting back into the precinct you find it impossible to discover the entrance to the car park.

This dream shows that you have a strong ability to store images and memories and reproduce them accurately.

Dream pattern 4

You are in a room with a solicitor, a policeman, a doctor, a newspaper reporter, an accountant, a tax inspector, a customs officer and a railway guard. They say nothing but stare at you with contempt. The silence is painful and the atmosphere glacial.

Fear of the future, the present and the past is crippling you. Your three basic problems are that you fear animals, yearn for excitement and dread any form of sexual encounter. Until you can come to terms with your feeling of insecurity you are unlikely to be able to combat these threats to your happiness.

Dream pattern 5

You are the leader of a large trade union and you spend your days and nights sitting on a throne surrounded by sycophantic aides and supporters. An endless stream of visitors come to pay homage to you but your pleasure in their tributes is spoilt by your awareness that you have soiled both yourself and the seat of your throne. You do not know how to stand up and leave the room without losing the respect of those around you.

What deep agonies lie behind this extremely common dream! Your fear of public humiliation has grown from your childhood days and your agonies are a result of your early exposure to violence and your numerous sexual misadventures.

Dream pattern 6

You are sitting alone in a small rowing boat, struggling to unravel a thousand yards of cheap string. It is raining hard and the boat is being buffeted by the wind and the waves. Just as you think you have found one end of the string the boat suddenly fills with thousands of writhing maggots.

Psychologists have argued for decades about the true meaning of this dream. Freud thought it was linked to an inner fear of emotional commitment, but Jung argued that Adler was right that the moment when the string turned into maggots signified a strong yearning for religious fulfilment. Pavlov disagreed with them all and suggested that the dream implied a fear of small boats and maggots.

What do objects in dreams mean?

If you dream of anything long and thin, long and thick, short and thin, short and thick, pointed, round, wet, warm, cavernous, blue, red, pink, purple, violet, white, brown, black, soft, hard, slender, broad, empty, full, slippery, stiff, mountainous, lumpy, hilly, fruity, tender, painful, rubbery, succulent, large, vast, breathtaking, impetuous, tantalising, tall, squat, wicked, evil, naughty, good, hot, bad, spicy, milky, nutritious, mobile, tasty. stationary, ardent, sweltering, sweating, simmering, flushing, smouldering, solid, firm, flexible, humid, damp, dewy, dripping or full then you are over-sexed.

If you dream of anything else at all then you are severely repressed. Your underlying urges are all sexually orientated, but you are sublimating them.

ACADEMIC MODULE SIXTEEN

Occupational Health

An introductory course in the dangers of employment

Whatever your job there is a real risk that it may be making you ill. The comprehensive directory and remedial suggestions which follow have been compiled with the aid of the Occupational Diseases Unit at the University of Hampstead on Sea.

Accountant

There is a real risk that you will bore yourself to death. Avoid this problem by spending one day every week tearing up income tax forms and scribbling obscenities on company ledgers.

Administrator

The only danger is that you will wake up one day and realise what you are doing for a living. Try not to ask yourself whether your daily tasks are satisfying or useful. Never wonder whether your current occupation matches up to the expectations you had when you were a teenager.

Bank clerk

Eczema on the chin caused by excessive salivation is a problem. There is also a risk of being killed or permanently crippled by a robber. Avoid this latter risk by handing over money quickly if the occasion demands.

Company director

Flying champagne corks can cause considerable damage. Some caviar is very salty and can exacerbate irregularities in blood pressure. Arthritis of the knee, caused by heavy secretaries, is another common problem.

Dentist

Fingers can be bitten off by patients. Overfilled wallets can produce sciatica.

Doctor

Suicide is a major risk in this occupation.

Factory worker

Few risks apart from chest, heart, skin, liver, kidney, lung, brain, bone, joint, bladder and nerve disorders.

Footballer

Likely to suffer from a wide range of bone and joint disorders: 'possible fracture', 'likely sprain' and 'conceivable bruise' are just three possibilities footballers have to face every time they play.

Lawyer

Remorse and bad conscience in later life can produce depression, anxiety and sleeplessness. (But who cares?)

Milkman

Nose injuries, venereal disease and shotgun wounds are the three most usual occupational hazards.

Policeman

Elbow and shoulder injuries are a common result of truncheons being wielded with too much enthusiasm. Over-indulgent rocking backwards and forwards can produce persistent dizziness. Megalomania is a major professional problem.

Taxi driver

A persistent sore throat is typical among people who drive cabs – together with strain-related injuries to the first two fingers of the right hand.

Typist

Typist's tit (caused by the carriage levers on old fashioned manual typewriters) is rare today. Typist's bottom caused by executives' fingers is still widespread.

Writer

Sore hands, sore fingers, sore elbows, malnutrition, hypothermia and a thousand and one other disorders are bravely faced and endured each day by the courageous men and women who selflessly devote themselves to the task of educating and entertaining their fellow creatures.

Administrative Management

Introductory course in counter-administration

Bureaucrat baiting: the art of annoying civil servants and administrators

Any life lived to the full will be bound to include regular bureaucrat baiting. Like the reproductive urge, it's a natural instinct and shouldn't be repressed. The suggestions for efficient baiting printed below are made primarily for those who have come late to this simple pleasure, or for anyone whose inventiveness is beginning to flag.

1 Write two letters saying precisely the opposite things and post them on the same day.

2 Ask for a copy of the official complaints procedure. Send your letter of request by recorded delivery.

3 Add an extra letter or an extra figure to the reference you're asked to quote on your replies.

4 Send one page of what is obviously a two page letter.

5 Enclose a cheque for a very small amount of money when no-one has asked you for any.

6 Make constant references to a previous letter that you never wrote.

7 Make constant references to a previous letter that they never wrote.

8 Add a postscript to your letter saying that you have sent a copy to Mr Hoskins. There doesn't have to be a Mr Hoskins, of course.

9 Enclose an invoice for £1.5 million with your letter and write MUST BE PAID IN SEVEN DAYS on it.

ACADEMIC MODULE EIGHTEEN

Obsequies and Exequies

Basic dying

Making arrangements

1   Remember that quite a lot of churches will organise 'self service' burials these days. You get the hire of a spade, a tape-recorded prayer, a box of paper tissues, a cardboard unisize casket, a set of black cotton armbands (washable) and a bunch of plastic lilies. Try to die within a few yards of your grave and all you'll need to provide are the mourners.

2   Cremation is still the best buy if you're looking for value for money. Once you've been certified dead by a doctor you can do this yourself for hardly any cost at all. Rent a barbecue set, an asbestos spit and funnel and a pay-for-what-you-burn pack of charcoal. Buy a plastic urn with matching lid. If you really don't want to go to the expense of buying an urn, you can spread the ashes yourself by fixing a fan near to the barbecue. Finally, of course, you can cut the cost of your arrangements even further by cremating yourself with a friend.

Be remembered!

Death tends to be a rather final event and there is a risk that after your demise you will be forgotten. Here are some ways in which you can ensure that your life will be remembered.

1 Commission a pyramid. Sandstone is best. You will need approximately 400 acres of land with good access roads. Hebrew slaves can be hired by the thousand from all good synagogues. Your pyramid should include a suite of well furnished rooms and a fully functioning curse to prevent desecration. A games room is optional.

2 Commission an erection which displays your good points to the full. Ideally you should be mounted although you might need special permission from the Department of Public Works for this.

3 Arrange to have a small public building or disease named after you. If the disease is likely to be contracted or disseminated then your chances of being remembered are approximately doubled.

4 Get stuffed.

Glossary

ABORTOIR: Place where abortions are carried out.

ABSINTHE: Heart drug (immortalised in the phrase 'absinthe makes the heart go faster').

ADAM'S APPLE: Eve and the serpent conspired to make Adam turn fruity. Unfortunately Adam had a twinge of conscience and the apple stuck in his throat.

AMBULANCE: Free taxi. You don't even have to pay for the telephone call.

ANIMAL MAGNETISM: Many apparently sensible individuals are excessively fond of animals such as cats, dogs and baboons. This is entirely due to the magnetism of the animals concerned. There is no known cure.

ANOREXIA: A way to cut down on grocery bills.

ANTI-CLIMAX: (See also Climax.) A number of things are known as anti-climactic. The list is led by such items as thick rubber contraceptives, long woollen vests, ringing telephones, policemen with flash lights, screaming children, alcohol, ringing, chiming or buzzing door bells, unpainted ceilings, bursting water beds, and the return home of one partner's legally intended spouse.

ANTISEPTIC: Perfumes widely used in hospitals, health centres, etc.

APATHY: Problem that really isn't worth bothering about.

APERIENT: See Opening medicine.

APPENDIX OPERATION: Any surgical procedure described in the last few pages of a textbook of surgery.

APPOINTMENT: Random meeting between doctor and patient.

AQUAPUNCTURE: When a tyre bursts and it is raining.

ARMPIT: Place where surgeons put amputated upper limbs (see also Legpit).

ATHLETE'S FOOT: Something to put in an athlete's running shoe.

BALLOON: One prick and it's gone (cf. Virginity).

BIRTH: The only cure for pregnancy.

BLEEDER: Anyone who parks his car in the space allocated to the senior consultant surgeon.

BLISTER: Convex, elevated skin patches which are produced naturally by a reaction between the skin and any hard object. Available from stationers, hardware stores, etc. in special 'blister packs'.

BLOOD PRESSURE: If it were not under pressure the blood would not move around the body. If the pressure is too high blood travels round the body too quickly causing giddiness. Getting the pressure just right is something for doctors to worry about.

BLOW UP CUSHION: Essential item for a visit to the doctor's surgery. (See also Sandwiches and Flask).

BLUSH: Sign of innocence and embarrassment. Usually applied artificially these days.

BOWEL: Useful container. Available in many different sizes.

CANCER: June 22 - July 22.

CASTOR OIL: Special, viscous liquid used for lubricating the tiny wheels underneath sofas, beds, arm chairs, and so on.

CATARACT: Large waterfall. The massive amount of spray makes it difficult to see clearly.

CERTIFICATE: Any small piece of paper containing a mixture of unreadable printing and illegible handwriting.

CHESTS: Because so many significant disorders affect the chest many doctors feel that no physical examination is complete without a thorough study of the chest. Studies show that females in their twenties are at particular risk from chest complaints. Consequently a number of practitioners confine their examinations of the chest to patients in this category.

CHICKENPOX: This disease has nothing to do with chickens

and nothing to do with the pox.

CHOLESTEROL: Substance blamed for all those disorders which have been shown to have no connection with smoking.

CLAVICLE: Old fashioned musical instrument made from human collar bone.

CLEAVAGE: The shadow of the valley of life.

CLIMACTERIC: Relating to weather.

CLOT: Politician.

COLD SPOTS: Aberdeen, Moscow, All of Iceland, Oslo, Manchester sometimes.

COMA: It is important to differentiate between 'coma' and 'death'. The best test is to hold a mirror up in front of the individual's face. All living persons will respond immediately. Women check their make up. Men examine their hair line.

CONFERENCE: Tax free holiday.

COUCH: Piece of furniture on which patients lie while being examined and starlets recline when being cast.

COURSE: Green area on which people play golf. When absent from their normal duties doctors will leave instructions with their secretaries that they are 'off on a course'. (Another popular ploy is to say that one is at a 'meeting' – forgetting to put the word 'race' before the word 'meeting'.)

CRICK: Small parasite which lives in the human neck and causes both pain and stiffness. (As in 'I've got a crick in my neck').

CRUTCH: Piece of equipment used to help drivers change gear in Japanese motor cars.

CROUP: To croup is to assist in a gaming room. Someone who does this for a living is a croupier.

CUP OF TEA (NICE): Essential first aid remedy. Should be made with plenty of milk and sugar and served piping hot. Suitable for all emergencies where the patient is conscious or a bystander is thirsty.

CURD: This is a misprint.

CYNIC: A patient who when told that his doctor is on a course believes that the doctor is playing golf.

CYSTITIS: Disease commonly affecting the skin of the female nose. Sufferers make frequent trips to the ladies room to 'powder their noses'.

DEGENERATION: Process which begins when a school boy or school girl enters Medical School.

DENTAL NURSE: Pretty young lady with large bust employed to distract the patients in a dentist's surgery.

DERBYSHIRE NECK: Piece of human anatomy which holds Derbyshire head onto Derbyshire body.

DIAGNOSIS: A guess or estimate made by anyone with recognised medical qualifications.

DIPLOPIA: Individuals suffering from diplopia have an irresistible desire to collect paper qualifications. The disease usually burns itself out in middle life. Diplopia is extremely common among young members of the medical profession.

DISLOCATION: Mental problems caused by moving house.

DIZZINESS: See Giddiness.

DOUBLE: Normal sized measure of alcohol.

DOUBLE VISION: Normally both eyes move together. If for any reason the eyeballs develop independent suspension double vision will follow.

DOUCHE: Intimate shower for one.

DRAUGHT: Piece or 'man' used in a popular board game.

DROPSY: Disease which is an occupational hazard among waiters and waitresses.

DROWNING: People drown because they swallow and inhale water. It is clear, therefore, that drowning could be avoided if people at risk kept their mouths shut.

DRUG COMPANY: Philanthropic organisation devoted to the production and distribution of matching pen sets, plastic name plates, prints of old fashioned sailing ships, diaries, calendars illustrated with photographs of Swiss chalets and blotting pads. Will also provide doctors and their wives with meals. May make and sell drugs in addition.

DRUGS: Medicinal and non medicinal substances taken by other people.

DYSENTERY: If you develop diarrhoea while abroad you are entitled to call it dysentery.

DYSLEXIA: Hrjkl mnjkr ljlkrt jhlmj prhky ljk j jkhrlm!

EAR-ACHE: This condition only ever occurs at night (usually at approximately 3 a.m.) and affects only young children. The remedy is to telephone the doctor straight away. By the time he arrives, sleepy and bad tempered, the child will once more be sleeping peacefully. Delaying the initial telephone call has little or no effect on the outcome.

EARS: Prominent, vestigial apparatus used by the short and long sighted as suitable projections on which to hang spectacles.

ELECTRIC SHOCK: Common four times a year in most households. Best remedy is perhaps to move every time a bill is due and to leave no forwarding address.

ENAMEL: Natural substance found in human teeth. Extracted by a complex chemical process and used for covering kettles, stoves, etc.

ENEMA: Inner cleansing with a vengeance. Once immensely popular with French monarchs. Still very popular with some retired Colonels whose needs are met by specialist nurses in Soho.

EPIDEMIC: As far as journalists on popular daily newspapers are concerned epidemics are diseases affecting two or more individuals living in approximately the same town at approximately the same time.

EUNUCH: Caretaker in Nurses' Home.

EVERYTHING: Source of all female problems; only removed in the last resort (as in 'She's had everything taken away').

EXERCISE: A common cause of injury and disease. To be avoided by all who wish to remain healthy. Those who insist on taking up exercise should begin by watching others on television. The truly slothful might begin their exercise programme by watching televised snooker, for example.

EXPECTANT MOTHER: Mother waiting for someone to offer to do the washing up.

EXPERT: Anyone who possesses slides and is prepared to travel a long distance.

EYEBROW: A well trained eyebrow can be used to express pleasure, surprise, shock, horror, pride, happiness and regret. Surgeons and nurses who wear masks while working in the operating theatre learn to converse with one another solely with the aid of their eyebrows.

FAITHFUL: A patient who believes that when his doctor is said to be on a course he is away studying is a faithful patient (cf. Cynic).

FATS: Affectionate first name for Black American vocalist and pianist, usually remembered for his rendition of the musical item 'Red Sails in the Sunset'.

FERTILE: A woman who has a baby that her husband or boyfriend did not expect or plan will always explain that she is exceptionally fertile.

FETISH: Fetishists obtain tremendous sexual pleasure from objects not always associated with sex. There are, for example, individuals with a fetish for female underwear while others get satisfaction from touching long hair. Some individuals enjoy foot fetishism and get their pleasure from shoes. Especially dainty black leather shoes. With high heels. And little buckles or bows. Fitting snugly around petite, white feet. No one enjoys his work more than a foot fetishist working in a shoe shop.

FIRST AID: A cup of tea, a glass of brandy and a rug are the first things which the apprentice first aider should learn to handle with confidence. Only later should the tin of plasters, safety pin, triangular bandage, bottle of congealed cough medicine, tube of rubbing liniment and calamine lotion be tackled.

FLASK: Essential item for a visit to the doctor's surgery. (See also Blow up cushion and Sandwiches).

FLATULENCE: North south wind.

FLOATING KIDNEY: The kidney is responsible for producing urine. The urine is then stored in the bladder. If production exceeds storage facilities there may be an embarrassing surfeit at the production site. When this happens a floating kidney may result.

FLOODING: When flooding occurs drowning may result. (See Drowning.)

FLU: Term widely used to describe cold symptoms which might not otherwise be treated seriously.

FLUSHING: A normal female condition. It is first noticeable in early teenage years. The phenomenon disappears during the years of motherhood but returns later in life.

FONDLE: To examine the female breast in a patient between the age of 16 and 30 (see also Grope).

FOOD POISONING: Disease made fashionable by Lucretia Borgia.

FOOT: Old fashioned unit of measurement approximately equal to the length of the average human shoe filler.

FRIAR'S BALSAM: Balsam belonging to a friar.

FRICTION RUB: Massage with a novel by a Japanese author.

FRUIT FARM: See Loony bin.

FUNNY FARM: See Fruit farm.

GANGRENE: Word derived from army slang. When referring to infected wounds soldiers would sometimes say to their colleagues 'it's gone green'. This slowly acquired status as a diagnostic label.

GAS SHOCK: cf. Electric shock.

GERM: Term of endearment for person of Teutonic extraction.

GERMAN MEASLES: Disease produced during first world war by German scientists as part of a plan to end the war quickly. The idea was to keep parents up at night looking after spotty children. This, it was thought, would cause anxiety and exhaustion, making British soldiers unable to fight.

GIDDINESS: See Dizziness.

GLANDS: Women have glands all over the place. There is nothing that can be done about them.

GLOVES: Doctors and surgeons sometimes wear these when touching and operating on patients to avoid leaving finger prints.

GRAND MAL: French for 'High Street' or 'Main Road'.

GRAVEL: Small stones found in driveways and bladders.

GRIPE WATER: Australian slang term for wine (as in 'Give us a glass of gripe water, cobber').

GROPE: Thorough medical examination usually performed on patient's relative, hospital visitor, secretary, etc., etc.

GUM: Lancashire God to whom all the Lancastrians pay allegiance (as in the oath 'Ee by Gum!').

IMPOTENCE: See Limp.

INDECISIVENESS: Probably nothing to worry about. Although if it persists it may be worth seeking advice.

INFERTILITY: The main consolation about this disorder is that it is only very rarely hereditary.

INGROWING TOE NAIL: Pain can usually be alleviated by wearing large comfortable shoes and limping.

INQUEST: Court hearing at which doctors who know nothing about the law appear before a lawyer who knows nothing about medicine to discuss the death of an individual none of them knew.

INSOMNIA: Insomnia is nothing much to worry about. It is certainly nothing that a good night's sleep won't put right.

IRIS: Girl who works in chemist's shop. Always has the top three buttons of her blouse unbuttoned and seems to be permanently anchored to the 'surgical sundries' counter.

JUGULAR: Individual who earns a living throwing several objects into the air and catching them in turn. Objects popularly used include balls, Indian clubs and knives.

JUNIOR HOSPITAL DOCTOR: Tired, thin and impotent person.

KEY WORDS: When doctors interview patients they listen for 'key words'. These tell the doctor what to do next. For example, if the doctor hears words such as 'football match', 'backache' or 'run down' he will immediately conclude that the patient simply wants a sick note. He will, therefore, reach for his pad of sick notes without further delay.

KIDNEYS: Essential small organs named after the metal dishes commonly used in hospitals which have a similar shape.

KINKY BOOTS: See Mammary hypertrophy.

KLEPTOMANIAC: Someone who has an uncontrollable, unreasonable affection for kleptos.

KNEE JERK: See Foot fetishist.

KNOCK KNEE: Doctors do this with a small rubber hammer. If the patient is alive and unparalysed there will naturally be some reaction.

LASSITUDE: Dog bitten.

LATIN: Swarthy looking man, usually a good dancer.

LAXATIVE: See Aperient.

LEGPIT: See Armpit.

LEMON: See Lime.

LIME: See Lemon.

LIMP: See Impotence.

LINT: Fluffy form of dressing, invented by someone with a nasty sense of humour. Sticks to everything.

LIPS: Neatly finished orifices are edged with lips. Males have one neatly finished orifice. Females have two.

LITHOTOMY POSITION: See *Kama Sutra*, p36.

LIVER FLUKE: Hepatic serendipity.

LOBOTOMY: Operation performed on patients who complain too much.

LOGORRHEA: Type of intestinal hurry which is endemic among lumberjacks.

LOIN: Area of the body which includes and surrounds the frayed or twiddly bits.

LOONY BIN: See Nut house.

LOUSE: Philanderer.

MALINGERING: Making a quick recovery from disabling symptoms and being able to watch the football match/fetch the mother in law from the airport/redecorate the kitchen/take the wife to the matinee/meet the girlfriend behind the bicycle sheds – and make good use of the doctor's sick note.

MAMMARY HYPERTROPHY: Big tits. (See also Kinky boots.)

MANDIBLE: Jawbone. The female mandible weighs 2.3 times as much as the male mandible.

MASK: Essential item of surgical clothing. Invariably worn by surgeons who wish to avoid recognition.

MASOCHISM: There is no need for treatment when this problem causes great concern.

MASSEUSE: A young lady who has specialised in using her hands to help relieve tension in men and release built-up pressures. Parts of the body which start off limp and flaccid will quickly become firm, swollen and taut before becoming limp and flaccid again. Most of the leading establishments employing masseuses are in big cities.

MASTOID: Anyone who is tall, thin and rather wooden is said to be mastoid.

MEDICAL SPOKESMAN (otherwise known as A. Doctor): Someone who knows absolutely nothing about anything and who is therefore expected to comment authoritatively on everything.

MEGALOMANIA: Disease which commonly affects hospital consultants. There is no known cure. Symptoms sometimes ameliorated by retirement.

MEMBER: A member is usually in something. More than that I am not prepared to say.

MENSTRUATION: There are two remedies for this: pregnancy and hysterectomy. The first of these (which has long lasting side effects) needs a man. The second needs a doctor.

MILK: Breast juice. As an adjunct to their main purpose (the entertainment of the male) the female breasts can be used as a source of cheap milk for feeding infants.

MINER'S ELBOW: Part of a miner.

MINER'S LUNG: Another part of a miner.

MINER SURGERY: Operation to remove a miner.

MINOR SURGERY: Operation to remove a small child.

MOLE: Small, friendly, furry creature which lives inside the skin and burrows to the surface occasionally, leaving small dark marks where the outer layer of skin has been disturbed.

MORNING SICKNESS: Early warning designed to give a woman notice that her contraceptive technique is not perfect.

MOUNTAIN SICKNESS: Volcanic eruption (usually occurs on a Sunday morning after a hectic Saturday night).

MOUTH BREATHING: This is only really a problem when carried out under water (see Drowning).

MUMPS: Natural form of birth control. The only form of birth control recommended by the Pope.

MURMURS: Have to be stopped as soon as possible. Even at an early stage they can do harm.

MYXOEDEMA: Disease caught from eating infected rabbit meat.

NERVE: What you need to talk back to the doctor's receptionist.

NIGHT BLINDNESS: Can be cured permanently (or at least until the batteries wear down) by buying a flash light.

NIPPLE: Tip of the iceberg.

NOTES: If your doctor has a one inch thick pile of notes about you it is probably a medical record.

NUT HOUSE: See Funny farm.

OPTIMIST: Someone who arrives five minutes early for a hospital appointment.

OSTEOPATH: Someone prepared to put his work into your back.

OTITIS: A fear of lifts.

PALPITATIONS: Best described as the feeling you get when you realise that you nearly walked out of a supermarket without paying.

PALSY: Friendly.

PANCREAS: Early Christian martyr who died of diabetes and was later made a Saint. A main line London railway station is named after him.

PATHOLOGIST: The only doctor who knows for sure that his patients will never complain.

PATIENTS: Individuals without whom all health care institutions would operate far more effectively and efficiently. It is entirely the fault of the patients that doctors' appointment systems fail to operate efficiently and that so much has to be spent on drugs, laundry, floor cleaning and swabs. Patients are also responsible for spoiling doctors' lunches and for increasing the need for hospital administrators. It is an indisputable fact that without patients, costs of running almost all hospital facilities could be cut by 7.5%

PAUNCH: Extremely useful part of the human body within which nutriments can be stored. The human paunch serves much the same sort of purpose as the camel's hump. People without paunches die much quicker when food is unavailable and therefore after the apocalypse the world will be entirely populated by people with paunches.

PERSONALITY: Anyone hired to open a hospital fête.

PHARMACIST: Anyone old enough to count, tall enough to reach the top shelf and in possession of a clean white coat.

PHLEBITIS: Latin name for small puncture marks made by tiny creatures which are renowned for their jumping skills.

PHOTOPHOBIA: Fear of being photographed by a hidden camera while undressing in a doctor's cubicle. More common than is widely thought especially since a survey showed that 37% of all doctors had cameras hidden in their light fittings.

PIGEON TOED: Having three toes pointing forward and one toe pointing backwards.

PINS AND NEEDLES: Small, long, thin, sharp metal instruments used in sewing, needlework, etc.

PLACENTA: Life support system for unborn babies.

PLASTER OF PARIS: French dressing.

PLUMBI OSCILLANS: Lead swinging.

PREGNANCY: Disease women catch from men. Transmitted by close personal contact.

PREMATURE BABIES: Any baby born less than nine months after the wedding of its parents is said to be premature. Because they are smaller, premature babies are easier to deliver. An Irishwoman, Mrs Bridie Murphy, who had eleven premature babies insisted that she was always grateful for small Murphys.

PREMENSTRUAL TENSION: The best remedies are hysterectomy and pregnancy. Any remaining anxiety can then be dealt with as ordinary anxiety.

PRICKLY HEAT: Condition caused by sharp, spiky rays of sunshine.

PROLAPSE: If this occurs a second time it is known as a relapse or a second coming down.

PUBERTY: Time when small girls stop being interested in dolls and boys start being interested in them.

PUBLIC RELATIONS: People who have sexual intercourse in parks, fields, lanes, telephone boxes, shop doorways, cars or steps of government buildings are said to be having 'public relations'.

PUNDIT: Anyone treated with deference by a television interviewer.

PURGATIVE: See Laxative.

PUSHING: The only time that it is ever considered acceptable to push is right at the end of a pregnancy. Polite pushing is therefore a female prerogative.

QUARANTINE: Period of time during which someone suspected of having something he shouldn't have is kept away from people who are anxious to ensure that they don't get what he might have got.

QUEER: Adjective used to describe an ill defined feeling of illness as in 'I feel a little queer'. Some of those who have uttered these words have found themselves in trouble with the authorities. (See also Public lavatory.)

QUESTIONS: Doctors ask many questions when talking to patients. Sometimes they ask the same questions more than once. It is important to understand that at this stage in the consultation the doctor is trying to decide which form of response is most suitable – certification or examination and treatment. He is, therefore, looking for key words (q.v.). Patients are not usually encouraged to ask questions of their own.

QUICK: Part of the nail to which nail biters aspire.

RADIOLOGIST: Anyone working in the X-ray department and earning more money than the senior radiographer.

RASHES: Some are infectious and some are not.

RAT: A single parent who doesn't know he is a single parent.

REPRESENTATIVE: Drug company employee. The only person who will sit in a doctor's waiting room for more than an hour when not ill. Doctors like drug company representatives because they are, on the whole, patient, sympathetic and attentive. Only after listening to a doctor's moans for twenty minutes will a representative open his briefcase and produce information about his company's latest product. The necessary prescribing information will usually be printed on the side of a ball point pen.

RESEARCH LABORATORY: An institution devoted to the search for new remedies for the treatment of diseases which may or may nor exist.

RESTAURANT COMPLEX: Fear of eating in public.

RHESUS BABY: All women of child bearing age should keep away from zoos which have monkeys. If zoo visits are unavoidable women should stand well back from the cages. Rhesus babies should then be avoided.

RIBS: Usually wrap the lungs. Superfluous ones are very tasty when served with a rich barbecue sauce. I suggest 1 part soya sauce, 2 parts tomato paste, 2 oz brown sugar, tablespoon of vinegar.

RICKETS: Wooden sticks used by Chinese cricket players.

RUBBER NECK: Individual who has a double jointed cervical spine. Rubber-necks make very good spies and criminals because they are able to look over their shoulders with considerable ease.

SADISM: Any sadist looking for comfort and companionship should find a masochist and leave him.

SANDWICHES: Essential item for a visit to the doctor's surgery. (See also Blow up cushion and Flask.)

SCROTUM: Small bag of skin attached as an evolutionary afterthought to the male body and designed to provide accommodation for the testicles for which there is no room in the main part of the corporal accommodation.

SHOCK: The best remedy for a case of shock is a nice cup of tea. A chat with the vicar may also prove helpful.

SINUSITIS: Type of writer's cramp.

SLEEPING SICKNESS: zzz zzzzz zz zzzz zz zzz zzz zzz zzz z z z zzz!

SLIDES: Skis. Experts travelling to foreign conferences will often carry their slides on the top of the car.

SLIMMING CLUBS: Fat people who are consistently unsuccessful at dieting should join a slimming club. They will be able to meet lots of other fat people and moan about how unhealthy thin people look. They will also be able to swap excuses for not dieting successfully.

SNIP: A bargain.

SNORING: Women whose husbands snore all night are advised to sew marbles into the backs of their husbands' pyjama jackets. This has no effect at all on the snoring but it makes the husband sleep without his jacket on. This in turn may then lead to activities which reduce the amount of time the husband spends sleeping.

SNUFFLES: Lovely little guinea pig who belonged to a neighbour of ours four or five years ago.

SPECIAL DELIVERY: Baby whose mother or father is related to a member of the Regional Health Authority, any hospital administrator, a consultant in any speciality, a porter, a nurse or nursing officer, a politician (local or national), a journalist, a trade union official, a hospital electrician, a member of a Community Health Council, or anyone who understands the official complaints procedure.

SPERM: Small wriggly thing much smaller than a tadpole. And physiologically fairly different. There are anatomical differences too. And tadpoles grow up differently. In fact sperm aren't really very much like tadpoles at all.

SPLEEN: Organ which is particularly well developed in critics of all kinds.

SPRAIN: If your doctor says you have a sprain he may suggest that you rest and consult this glossary again in seven days if there is no improvement.

STARCH: Substance which converts some (but not all) limp things into crisp things capable of standing up for themselves.

STARVATION: Living on a very low protein, low fat, low carbohydrate diet.

STATISTICS: Any collection of figures that can be used to prove two opposing arguments at the same time.

STERILITY: Generally speaking people who suffer from sterility wish they didn't while people who don't wish they did.

STING: The 'sting' always comes right at the end of a consultation. When patients apply the 'sting' they usually preface it with phrases such as 'By the way…' or 'While I'm here…'.

They then proceed to introduce a complex, lengthy problem into a consultation which the doctor thought he had terminated. The new problem, to be truly classified as a 'sting', should ideally require the doctor to perform a full medical examination. When doctors apply the 'sting' they usually wait until the patient is actually touching the door handle. Then they say things like 'And, of course, no alcohol for six months' or 'Naturally you mustn't resume normal relations with the wife until I see you again. Make an appointment for three months time'.

STOOL: Small three-legged chair.

SUFFOCATION: Best treated with plenty of fresh air.

SUNSTROKE: Disease common among citizens from sunless nations who are visiting foreign countries where natural sunshine is available out of doors.

SUSPENDERS: Available in a wide variety of colours but the best ones are black. Included here for absolutely no valid reason at all. Except that it's a word some people like looking at.

SWOLLEN GLANDS: Mammary hypertrophy, or big tits.

TABLET: Large piece of stone on which message is written.

TATTOO: Noise the rain makes when it hits an iron roof. Because of the popularity of this type of roofing material in parts of Scotland the word 'tattoo' has become popularly associated with the Scottish capital.

TELEPHONE: The only medical instrument under the control of patients and likely to cause pain to doctors.

TENNIS NECK: To avoid this it is wise to sit behind the server rather than on the side lines.

THERMOMETER: Instrument used to silence talkative patients.

THRUSH: Garden song bird which carries an infective organism. It is thought that the infection is transmitted to humans when the bird lands on underwear drying on the washing line. This theory has not yet been substantiated.

THUMB: Overweight rather stocky finger which has independent suspension.

TIBIA: Greek Goddess who was, according to the writers of many ancient myths, responsible for looking after the shin bone.

TIREDNESS: Normal state of health for all individuals over the age of 16.

TONGUE DISCOLORATION: You should ring your doctor straight away if your tongue is discoloured. A discoloured tongue should not be put back into the mouth until it has been examined by a doctor.

TONSILS: Source of great wealth for some surgeons. Current rate of exchange is 12 pairs of tonsils to one detached house.

TOOTHACHE: A type of pain. Most cases can be cured by telephoning the dentist's surgery for an appointment. Sitting in the dentist's waiting room for five minutes will clear away any remaining pain in almost all cases.

TRAVEL SICKNESS: Many remedies have been tried. The expert we consulted suggested buying a large roll of brown paper. Before each trip cut off a piece of paper approximately 24" x 12". The paper should be folded into a square and the two sides sealed with sticky tape. This can then be kept on the lap throughout the journey. At the end of the trip the top of the bag can be sealed with sticky tape. On public transport the sealed bag can then be left hidden behind a cushion or in some other suitable spot. Alternatively, stay at home.

TREMOR: Hand shake which doesn't stop when the introductions are over.

TRENCH FOOT: Part of the body visible below bottom edge of trench coat.

ULCERS: Ulcers used to be treated with a mixture of milk and steamed fish. This treatment was easy enough to manage when the ulcers were inside the body (e.g. in the stomach) but the treatment could be very messy when the ulcers were on the outside of the body (e.g. a leg).

VAGINA: Watch this space.

VARICOSE VEIN: Surface blemish common among female intellectuals who traditionally try to disguise the problem by wearing blue stockings.

VARIETY THEATRE: An operating suite in which many different types of procedure are carried out.

VERTIGO: This is a condition that makes vertical people want to become horizontal people.

VIRGIN: Cf. Balloon.

WASTE-LAND: Area around the navel.

WASTING DISEASE: This disorder only affects people living in the developed countries. In some areas it is endemic. Signs of the disease include packets of food half eaten, clothes discarded before being worn out and the building of large dumps made up of outdated but perfectly functional fridges, cookers, washing machines, toasters, cars and bicycles.

WORRIED LOOK: Doctors often have worried looks. This isn't anything to worry about. It usually means that the doctor doesn't know your name. Try introducing your own name, age and address into the conversation as subtly as possible. You should soon see a look of relief replace the worried look.

WRINKLE: Small tip or piece of advice about skin care.

WRITER'S CRAMP: Abdominal pain caused by hunger. This cramp is usually only relieved by the appearance of royalty cheques.

WRY-NECK: A term used to describe someone who is exceptionally sharp, witty and cynical. See also Rubber-neck.

WEANING: Should always be completed before children leave home. The social problems associated with breast feeding children at boarding school can prove difficult to accept.

WHITLOW: A place in Ireland where infections of the finger are common.

WITCH HAZEL: Flying broomstick.

WOMB SERVICE: Cleansing of the uterus.

Appendix

The vermiform appendix is a vestigial structure. It is absent altogether in some carnivores whereas it is larger and more important in herbivores. A slender diverticulum of the large intestine, it is attached on the postero-medial aspect of the caecum. It can be found about one inch below the ileocaecal valve. The appendix is described as a 'vermiform' because it usually resembles a medium sized earthworm. It can however vary in length from a mere fragment of an inch to a full nine inches. In the foetus and the infant, the appendix projects from the lower end of the caecum. During childhood the position of the appendix is changed because of the unequal growth of the caecum. In adulthood the appendix most commonly lies behind the caecum. It may hang down into the pelvis. A small triangular mesenteric sheet, the meso-appendix attaches the appendix to the ilial mesentery.

You can find your own appendix by looking for the three taeniae coli. These converge at the root of the appendix and therefore act as a collective pointer.

And finally...

Now that you have finished this book you are entitled to a FREE diploma confirming that you have learned absolutely nothing of value and have therefore achieved degree status. You can now put the letters M.D. (Mildly Deranged) after your name. To obtain your official diploma send a large, self-addressed, stamped envelope together with a cheque for $1,750 (to cover postage and packing) to:

Sir Ramick Hobbs (Administrator)
Ever Open University Hall
c/o Dulverton Open Prison
Exmoor
Devon
England

Published by the European Medical Journal

Food for Thought

Your guide to healthy eating

Vernon Coleman

Packed with easy-to-use, up to date, practical information, *Food for Thought* is designed to help you differentiate between fact and fantasy when planning your diet. The book's 28 chapters include:

- Food the fuel: basic information about carbohydrates, protein, fat, vitamins and minerals
- When water isn't safe to drink—and what to do about it
- How what you eat affects your health
- Why snacking is good for you
- The mini-meal diet and the painless way to lose weight
- Quick tips for losing weight
- The Thirty-Nine Steps to Slenderness
- 20 magic superfoods that can improve your health
- The harm food additives can do
- 20-point plan for avoiding food poisoning
- Drugs and hormones in food
- Food irradiation, genetically altered food, microwaves
- 30 common diseases—and their relationship to what you eat
- How to eat a healthy diet
- 21 reasons for being a vegetarian
- How much should you weigh?
- How to deal with children who are overweight

ISBN 0 9521492 6 5
192pp   paperback   £9.95

Available from Book Sales, European Medical Journal, PO Box 30, Barnstaple, Devon EX32 9YU. Please write for a catalogue.

Published by the European Medical Journal

Bodypower

The secret of self-healing

Vernon Coleman

A new edition of a book that hit the Sunday Times and Bookseller 'Top Ten' charts.

- How your body can heal itself
- How your personality affects your health
- How to use bodypower to stay healthy
- How to stay slim for life
- How to conquer 90% of all illnesses without a doctor
- How to improve your eyesight
- How to fight cancer
- How to use bodypower to help you break bad habits
- How to relax your body and your mind
- How to use bodypower to improve your shape
- •• and much, much more! ••

What they said about the first edition:
☞ Don't miss it! Dr Coleman's theories could change your life
Sunday Mirror
☞ If you've got Bodypower, you may never need visit your
doctor again, or take another pill! *Slimmer*
☞ A marvellously succint and simple account of how the body
can heal itself without resort to drugs *Spectator*
☞ Could make stress a thing of the past *Woman's World*
☞ Shows you how to listen to your body *Woman's Own*
☞ Could help save the NHS from slow strangulation
The Scotsman

ISBN 0 9521492 8 1 160pp paperback £9.95
*Available from Book Sales, European Medical Journal, PO Box 30,
Barnstaple, Devon EX32 9YU. Please write for a catalogue.*

Published by the European Medical Journal

Relief from IBS

Simple steps for long-term control

Vernon Coleman

- Causes and symptoms of Irritable Bowel Syndrome
- The two-step control programme
- How you should change your diet
- How to look after your digestive system
- Relief from wind
- Watch out for foods that make your symptoms worse
- Stand up for yourself
- Build up your self-confidence
- Learn to relax your body and mind
- How worrying more can help you worry less
- Tips to help you cope with stress
- Take control of your life

1 898947 03 1
128pp   paperback   £9.95

Available from Book Sales, European Medical Journal, PO Box 30, Barnstaple, Devon EX32 9YU. Please write for a catalogue.

Published by the European Medical Journal

The Parent's Handbook

Your child's health

Vernon Coleman

(Includes advice from *The Traditional Home Doctor*)

- Is your baby developing properly?
- First aid, home nursing, and when to call the doctor
- Measles, mumps, chickenpox and more
- Average height/weight tables for children
- How to deal with a crying baby
- Breast and bottle feeding, weaning, and the faddy eater
- Asthma, diabetes, eczema, epilepsy, meningitis and more
- Children under stress and starting school
- Anorexia, hyperactivity, stuttering and more
- Ten basic rules of parenthood

1 898947 02 3
192pp paperback £9.95

Available from Book Sales, European Medical Journal, PO Box 30, Barnstaple, Devon EX32 9YU. Please write for a catalogue.

Published by the European Medical Journal

Mindpower

How to use your mind to heal your body

Vernon Coleman

A new edition of this bestselling manual

- A new approach to health care
- How your mind influences your body
- How to control destructive emotions
- How to deal with guilt
- How to harness positive emotions
- How daydreaming can relax your mind
- How to use your personal strengths
- How to conquer your weaknesses
- How to teach yourself mental self defence
- Specific advice to help you enjoy good health
- • and much, much more! • •

What they said about the first edition:

☞ Dr Coleman explains the importance of a patient's mental attitude in controlling and treating illness, and suggests some easy-to-learn techniques *Woman's World*

☞ An insight into the most powerful healing agent in the world—the power of the mind *Birmingham Post*

☞ Based on an inspiring message of hope *Western Morning News*

☞ It will be another bestseller *Nursing Times*

ISBN 1 898947 00 7
256pp paperback £9.95

Available from Book Sales, European Medical Journal, PO Box 30, Barnstaple, Devon EX32 9YU. Please write for a catalogue.

For a full catalogue of Vernon Coleman's books
please write to Publishing House, Trinity Place,
Barnstaple, Devon. EX32 9HJ. England.
Telephone (01271) 328892. Fax (01271) 328768